YOUR INNER EVE

YOUR

Discovering God's

INNER

Woman Within

EVE

The Reverend

DR. SUSAN NEWMAN

ONE WORLD   BALLANTINE BOOKS   *New York*

A One World Book
Published by The Random House Publishing Group
Copyright © 2005 by Reverend Doctor Susan Newman

www.oneworldbooks.net

Grateful acknowledgment is made to the following for
permission to reprint previously published material:

National Sexual Violence Resource Center:
State and territory sexual assault coalitions list compiled
by the National Sexual Violence Resource Center.
Reprinted courtesy of the National Sexual Violence Resource Center.

Tyndale House Publishers: Scripture quotations from *The Daily Walk Bible,
King James Edition*, copyright © 1988 by Tyndale House Publishers, Inc.
Reprinted by permission of Tyndale House Publishers, Inc.,
Wheaton, Illinois 60189. All rights reserved.

Library of Congress Cataloging-in-Publication Data

Newman, Susan D.
Your inner Eve : discovering God's woman within / Susan Newman.— 1st ed.
p. cm.
Includes bibliographical references.
ISBN 0-345-45080-9
1. Christian women—Religious life.   2. Women—Biblical teaching.   I. Title.
BV4527.N495 2005
248.8'43—dc22   2004054762

Manufactured in the United States of America

2   4   6   8   9   7   5   3

First Edition: February 2005

Text design by Laurie Jewell

This work is dedicated to all the women who
had an original thought, an idea, a philosophy, a prayer,
an answer, a solution, a resolve, a cure, a miracle, a vision,
and a new way—but were not allowed to speak. This work
is also dedicated to the numerous, nameless women
who refused to be silenced.

In Memory of

The Reverend Dr. Prathia L. Hall
Lisa Sullivan

ACKNOWLEDGMENTS

As always, I am thankful to God for all the blessings and lessons that have come my way. I also thank God for giving me a mother who—even though she does not clearly understand when I say, "Mom, I have a job"—is always supportive and loving. "Hey kid" to my sister, Connie, who entertains me with weekly stories about Lulu, my poodle niece. I'm grateful for the creativity and hard work of the Ballantine/One World family—thank you, Melody Guy, for being a brave editor who pushed me to write more after I'd said, "But I'm finished."

I've been blessed with a caring cicle of sisterfriends who have midwifed me through this publishing journey—TaRessa Stovall, Michelle N-K Collison, Nikki Mitchell, and Djana Pearson-Morris. I cannot forget you, Jarrett and godesigngroup .com, for creating my wonderful Web site—www.sincerely susan.com. Thank you, Steve White, for your inspiration through this project. Love to my Newman and Dabney family for continuous prayers and support. Thank you to Charlene

Hamilton, my administrative assistant, who unknowingly smoothed my days out with humor after I'd experienced difficult nights of writing.

Thank you to the readers everywhere. This book would not exist without the questions and e-mails from thousands of African American women I've met at churches, retreat centers, and book signings. I want to thank all bookstores for selling *Oh God!*, especially the independently owned African American bookstores and book clubs. Mad love goes out to SisterSpace Books in DC; Pyramid Art and Books, Little Rock, Arkansas; Karibu Books, Bowie, Maryland; Medu Books, Atlanta, Georgia; Eso Won, Los Angeles; Sibanye, Baltimore, Maryland; and Black Expressions.

My extreme gratitude and continued prayers for all the men and women (you know who you are) who shared their stories of horror, pain, struggle, faith, and victory so others may know that they are not alone in their present situations, and help is available to change and empower their lives.

My life continues to be enriched and sustained by the friendship of Joye Brown Toor, TaRessa Stovall, the Reverend Joe Johnson, the Reverend Dr. Leah Gaskin-Fitchue, the Reverend Graylan Hagler, the Jones and Davis family of DC/Maryland, Calvin Green, Dr. Yvonne Wilson, and especially my Smooth and Easy Hand Dance Family, Washington, DC. If your name is not on this page, it is only because you asked me not to put it here—but you know how much you mean to me. Always remember to love, forgive, laugh, and dance—this is our life, let's celebrate daily. As Teena Marie sings, "Miracles need wings to fly." You have been my miracle along the way. Thank you.

Blessings, Peace, and Love,
Susan

CONTENTS

A MUST-READ INTRODUCTION

Last week I attended a revival service in Washington, DC. After worship, standing in the vestibule of the church, an African American woman in her late thirties approached me, smiling. She said, "You don't know me, but I testify often about how you transformed my life." With excitement in her eyes like a child meeting Santa Claus for the first time, she shared her testimony with me. Last summer I preached at an afternoon worship service she attended. After the service I autographed copies of *Oh God! A Black Woman's Guide to Sex and Spirituality*. She was one of the people I shook hands with. When she looked down at my sandaled feet, she was amazed to see that I wore red polish on my toenails.

Now, I must admit initially it seemed strange that my wearing of red toenail polish could have such a profound impact upon a woman's life, but after she finished sharing and walked away it dawned on me that this was a woman who was raised to believe that there are certain things women of Spirit do not do, do not say, and ways good churchgoing women do not dress. So when she saw an ordained minister preaching the powerful Word of God with red toenail polish—it struck a chord in her heart. For the first time she believed it was all right for her to polish her toenails. This may seem like a minor breakthrough to some, but for this woman it was an epiphany. She had an inner desire to adorn herself with toenail polish, but believed it was forbidden or inappropriate for a Christian.

An epiphany is our personal "Aha!" moment. It is that time in your eternity when the lightbulb comes on in your head and heart. A mystery is solved, a riddle is unraveled, and all the pieces of the puzzle finally come together for you. I wrote *Your Inner Eve* so that, like this sister, you, too, might have a much-needed epiphany.

There are women in this world who are very successful by society's standards. They have the house, the car, the job, but there is still something missing. There is always that inner feeling of incompleteness, emptiness, self-doubt, and sometimes self-hatred. What could be causing these feelings? Most would say low self-esteem, but I think there is a bit more to it than that. Have you ever had a sense that there is more to you than you've realized? Have you ever felt there was another you—not a "Mini Me," but another expression of yourself—that has yet to be unleashed inside? Can you picture a part of yourself, sitting with her hands folded neatly in her lap, her mouth taped shut, waiting for permission from you to speak?

There *is* someone else inside you, and I'd like to call her your

Inner Eve. Yes, Eve, God's *original woman*, inside you. There is an "original you," the feminine expression of God's Spirit residing inside. She is the keeper of our self-esteem, our intuition, our creative nature. She is our best self, our champion, our protector. She is not afraid, she is not ashamed, she is strong, and she knows it. When we were little girls, Eve was the part of us that laughed out loud, played dress-up, didn't care if she beat the boys in games, and was willing to try almost anything once. On summer nights, she caught lightning bugs in a jar. On wintry mornings, she blew her breath on the cold windowpane. She believed in Santa Claus and the Tooth Fairy, and every time she saw the movie *Peter Pan* she clapped hard and loud for Tinker Bell to survive. When we were young and innocent, Eve was strong.

Many of us have lost touch with our Inner Eve through various experiences in our lives. Things happen that affect how we view ourselves and the world around us. We think differently about who we are, and our value and worth. Our self-esteem has been attacked. Our core beliefs have shifted. Our Eve has been silenced. Self-esteem can be hard to define. It is more than just feeling good about ourselves, taking pride in our accomplishments, or liking what we see in the mirror; self-esteem relates to the way we judge our own worth. It is looking at ourselves and seeing something valuable.

I believe in order to discover God's WomanSpirit, Eve, residing within, we must trust our own spiritual intuition and allow our rational mind to become a friend to our intuition,

not a foe. We have been taught to view these two as diametri-
cally opposed to each other. When we do not fully use both our
rational mind and our spiritual intuition together, however, we
are left with a spiritual blind spot. We can see in front of us, behind us, on our left and right. We can see what is over our
heads and under our feet, but we cannot always *sense* the presence and guidance of Spirit that surrounds us. God's Spirit is
available to aid and guide us through life, but we must give our
inner consent by closing our minds to negative, self-destructive
thoughts, and opening our minds to positive, loving new possibilities. Our own minds can be seen as a garden—a place where
the seeds of ideas are planted, nurtured, and cared for by us.

Each chapter of this book reveals an aspect of your Inner
Eve: Eve Recovered, Eve Powered Up!, Eve Acting Up!, Eve
Speaking Up!, Eve's Epiphany, Eve Renewed, and Eve Inspired.
At the end of each chapter is an Inward Reflection designed to
assist you in reflecting upon how to apply what you've read to
the development of your Inner Eve and the creation of a spiritual place within for nuturing yourself. In addition, you will be
given a "Susanism"—a short affirmation to remember from
that chapter.

As I wrote certain chapters, I realized that you may want information readily at hand relating to the topics I've addressed.
The Resource Guide is included to provide you with a starting
point for gathering information. It is my hope that as you read
the book, your mind will be stimulated to do something about
domestic violence and women; or you may need to speak to

someone about your own situation. I want to provide a ready list of places you can contact for assistance.

I included a section on faith-based curricula on sexuality for children, youths, and adults. Over the years, as I've conducted faith-based teen pregnancy and HIV/AIDS education and prevention trainings, I've found that most people do not know where to look for current materials. There are excellent materials available for the faith community that teach adults how to begin the conversation about our sexuality as a gift from God. There are materials age-appropriate for everyone from preschool children to adults. Various denominations have produced these resources, including Catholics, Presbyterians, United Methodists, United Churches of Christ, and the Black Church Initiative of the Religious Coalition for Reproductive Choice, whose stellar programs "Keeping It Real!" and "Breaking the Silence" have gotten the African American church's youths talking to their parents about the responsibilities of sexuality.

My wish for you is that you claim your power, find your voice, and do something that is a blessing not only in your life, but in the lives of others as well.

I want to hear from you, too. You may contact me through my Web site at www.sincerelysusan.com. Let me know what you think about the book, and share your experiences while discovering God's original woman within. Now get to reading; there's a whole new world just waiting for your Inner Eve.

YOUR
INNER
EVE

Chapter One

EVE, WHERE ARE YOU?

EVE RECOVERED

God did not make us to be eaten up by
anxiety, but to walk erect, free, unafraid
in a world where there is work to do,
truth to seek, love to give and win.

—JOSEPH FORT NEWTON

I received an e-mail one day that contained humorous stories about children in a Catholic elementary school. One child said, "The first commandment was when Eve told Adam to eat the apple." This child's understanding of the story is indeed humorous. But upon rereading the creation story recorded in Genesis chapters 1 and 2, I've started thinking about Eve and what she must have been thinking when she ate the fruit. First, though, let's look at the fact that there are two creation stories.

The first one is found in Genesis 1:26–27: "And God said, Let us make man in our image, after our likeness; and let them have dominion over the fish of the sea, and over the fowl of the air, and over every creeping thing that creepeth upon the earth. So God created man in his own image, in the image of God created he him; male and female created he them." It is the sixth day, and God has been working all week long creating the world—speaking light into existence, separating the waters from the waters, and making firmament (whatever that is).

Now God makes humanity in God's own image—male and female. They both are given dominion over all things. There are no instructions about not eating from a particular tree. There is no language of husband and wife—it's all good in God's eyes, just be fruitful and multiply.

Then, in Genesis 2:2, God has finished working and rested on the seventh day. But things shift by verse 7—God is making man again out of the ground. "And the Lord God formed man out of the dust of the ground and breathed into his nostrils the breath of life, and man became a living soul." God then creates Eve from Adam's side. God commands them not to eat of the fruit of the tree of knowledge of good and evil.

What happened? Was God dreaming when God made them equals yesterday? Something must have happened that we are not privy to, because here on the eighth day there is a different creation story. This time there's talk about husband and wife, and leaving mother and father, cleaving and becoming one. Where did mothers and fathers come from? God is the only parent Adam and Eve have known—there are no other people on earth. Maybe Moses had too much palm wine when he wrote this section, I don't know. But I do remember that as a young seminarian, I learned that according to the Hebrew tradition Adam's first wife was Lilith, who was his equal. She was a very liberated woman and did not like the way Adam was doing things, so she left the Garden. Let's just say, she wasn't interested in being a "helpmeet" for Adam. So this second wife, Eve, is created not equal to Adam, yet a part of him. Trust me, every theologian, minister, prophet, and priest will have his or her own interpretation and explanation of the creation story. Remember, some folks believe we evolved from primates. Still, whether you see this as two stories, or one story with a follow-up detailed summary, the impact throughout the ages has been the same—Eve has borne the blame for "original sin."

She was tempted to eat from the forbidden tree by the serpent, and she did eat. She also gave fruit to Adam, and he did eat. Their eyes were opened; they became fully aware of their nakedness and covered themselves with fig leaves. Later, when God came looking for them, God called out, "Adam, where are you?" They both were hiding from God among the trees. Adam answered, "I heard thy voice and I was afraid because I was naked." Then the inquiry began, when God asked Adam what had happened. Adam answered, "This woman you gave me offered me the fruit, and I did eat." Eve explained that the serpent fooled her. Then God cursed the snake to be under the foot of humanity, man to toil the earth for his food and live by the sweat of his brow, and woman to suffer under the rule of her husband and to endure sorrow in childbirth. They were banished from the Garden, and an angel with a flaming sword was set at the gate as a barrier.

There are a lot of messages here. For me, it's important to note that Eve should not bear the weight of this original sin thing alone. God gave Adam dominion over all animals; he even named them. So when the serpent started speaking to Eve, questioning God's instructions to her about the tree,

Adam should have interrupted the slithering thing and said, "Shut your lying mouth!" Adam was standing there when this was going on. He wasn't off in the western section of Eden—he was standing right there. He could have nipped this whole thing in the bud. Look at the text. Genesis 3:6 says, "And when the woman saw that the tree was good for food, and that it was pleasant to the eyes, and a tree to be desired to make one wise, she took of the fruit, and did eat, and gave also unto her husband with her; and he did eat."

Adam was out of place. I'm speaking not of his geographic location, but his spiritual authority. God gave him instructions concerning how things should be in the Garden, as well as dominion over all animals. Adam was the "point man," but he was out of place. He stood there and said nothing. Nor did he do anything to silence the snake, or try to reason with Eve about her dialogue and subsequent actions. Most women, even though we have chosen a certain train of thought or action, will engage in reflection and dialogue if someone initiates the conversation. The snake continued to talk, while Adam was silent. So original sin is not solely an Eve event, but we can learn some things from this story.

DON'T TALK TO SNAKES

In Genesis 3:1, we are already told by the narrator that the serpent was more subtle than any beast of the field that God had created. The snake was, in the words of a 1970s song, "sly, slick

and wicked." His main agenda that day was to upset the equi-
librium in Adam and Eve's Garden. I don't know why he approached Eve instead of Adam, but I have my assumptions.
First, I think the snake came to Eve because she would notice
him. He was a very beautiful creature; he would catch her eye
and hold her attention. There was no fear in the Garden, no
reason to avoid any animal. Second, the snake must have
known that woman is a very engaging, thinking, and conversa-
tional human—he could entertain Eve with his notions about
the tree for discussion, consideration, and deduction.

But what we learn from this conversation is that when Eve
began to talk to the snake, her life began a downward spiral.
Up to that moment, things were good for her. She was God's
original woman, living in the peace and plenty of a beautiful
garden, no fear, no doubts, no shame, and no bra and girdle!
Then she talked with the snake. The first jewel of wisdom we
learn is: *Don't talk to snakes*. There are always people whose
very nature is to deceive you, make you doubt your best mind,
and make choices that are not in your best interest. Mark
Twain once said, "Keep away from people who try to belittle
your ambitions. Small people always do that, but the really
great make you feel that you, too, can become great."

Our lives in some form or fashion offer us the beauty, serenity, and comfort of a garden—and then we allow snake-like
folk to influence our minds. We allow toxic thoughts to enter
into our peaceful world through conversations, suggestions,
and so-called advice. We can't afford to talk to snakes. Snakes

are people who are dangerous, deadly, and deliberately decep-
tive. They want only to direct our downfall, annihilate our
achievements, and obliterate our accomplishments. We cannot afford to commune with these conspirators, ponder their
thoughts, consider their suggestions, or listen to their lies. A
snake-like person is a bitter person. These are usually small-
minded people who only get joy out of blocking someone else's
progressive life. If they cannot be stars of the show, then there
can be no show. If they cannot get what they want, they hate
to see anyone else fulfilled and unfortunately will seek to make
your life miserable. You know the old adage: "Misery loves
company." The result of such encounters is always a breakdown
in our spirits, our growth, and our self-worth. But you have
help closer than you think—your Inner Eve.

It is possible to have strong and healthy self-esteem when
we are aware of our Inner Eve. Taking an honest look at ourselves is often the best way to evaluate who we are, where we
are, and where we want to go. Ask yourself, *What do I want?* We
need a way of handling the little day-to-day setbacks to our
sense of security and significance. It all starts with our thinking. We have to retrain ourselves to think of *what is true about
me*. Our spirits are very fragile, easy to break, but not impossible to repair. Low self-esteem makes us our own worst enemy.

The most basic need all of us have is for a sense of personal
worth. Our sense of personal worth is based on the security of
knowing we are loved and accepted for who we are, regardless
of what we do. In addition, our personal worth is hinged on our

significance in this world: having meaning or purpose in our lives, and knowing that we are good at what we do in life. The formation of this sense of fundamental value begins in our childhood. Unfortunately, it can be affected by many things— constant ridicule, harsh words, unloving actions. All tear away at a child's sense of value, resulting in an adult's insecurity about herself.

To this very day, my mother cannot ask me, "What did you eat for dinner?" without me cringing. I have been fighting a battle with my weight since I was five years old. I remember Momma taking me to the doctor's office, where the two of them talked about my weight and what to do. Each morning I woke up to half a grapefruit, a boiled egg, and a dry piece of toast, or sometimes cereal and skim milk. But thank God for Sunday! Momma worked on Sundays, and our babysitter, Mrs. Phillips, cooked grits, scrambled eggs, and bacon for breakfast. Momma made special desserts on Monday, her day off from work. So we could always look forward to a chocolate cake, bread pudding, or rice pudding on Monday after school. Food became an issue early in my life.

Even though I was fat, I would still run, jump, and play like the other kids until they started giving me messages that something was wrong with me, something was different. Some of the "bad" boys at school called me pork chop or fatso. Not only the children, but also the adults joked about my weight. One teacher called me Butterball. She even had a little jingle to go with the name: "Here comes little Butterball, she's as round as she is tall." At home my plate was watched, at school my body was ridiculed, and inside Eve was holding little Susie's hand and wiping her tears.

A child constantly hearing these criticisms and negative words internalizes them, and they can become part of her view of herself. The tape in her mind plays the messages back as significant information learned from her parents, peers, and other adults. I grew up to be an overachiever with the voice of my critics' disapproval ringing in my ears. The child within is now inhabiting an adult body. My early messages were that I would be loved more if I were not fat; that fat people were not good enough or smart enough; that something was wrong with us. So my entire life I've been gaining and losing the same sixty pounds while getting straight A's in school, graduating at the top of my class, finishing college with honors and a double major, winning scholarships to study in Europe, achieving every goal, breaking barriers as a woman in the ministry, and still cringing when my mother asks me, "What did you eat for dinner?"

We often develop false notions of what we think will make us lovable, acceptable, and worthy. We believe we will be loved and accepted if we lose or gain weight. We will be okay if we change our hair by cutting it, growing it, locking it, or bone-straightening it. All we need to do is take more classes, read another book, learn to meditate, or learn to cook. We will be all right—*just let me consult with Oshun,* or *take another spiritual bath,* or *check in with the position of the moon.* We'll get a personal trainer and a life coach, our teeth we will whiten, and no more will we smoke. But alas, after all we've sacrificed and worked to achieve, the only voice we really need to hear is the voice of our Inner Eve.

DON'T GIVE YOUR FRUIT AWAY

In the Garden of Eden, Eve gave her fruit to Adam. It is a woman's natural inclination to share what she has with her man. Even more so for Eve, since she and Adam were the only two people in the Garden. You know how it is when you go out to dinner with your husband or boyfriend and you order something that is sooooooooooooo good. You smack your lips and lean toward him with a bit of food on your fork saying, "Here, taste this, it is so good." That's what Eve did. But unfortunately, by doing so, she made a choice that was not what God desired for her life.

Why did she choose to eat the fruit? Yes, the snake enticed her, but she made the decision to eat it. No one really knows what was going on in her head and heart at the time, but I can speculate that Eve was the first person who had to grapple with the issue of free will. God did not make us as computerized robots, programmed to do specific things. God made us in God's image and likeness with free will to decide how we shall live and be in relationship with God and each other. God still shows us God's will, and then allows us to choose our paths in this life. We have Eve's example as a lesson to always follow the guidance of Spirit when we are called to make choices.

Sisters, don't give your fruit away. Right or wrong, live your own life, follow your own mind, and listen to the wisdom of what Spirit is telling you. Yes, others may advise, but you decide. If your decisions about how you live your life, walk your path, grow your Garden do not meet the expectations of others—*tough*! You have to be led by what Spirit is telling you, showing you, and giving you. If you make great strides—they are yours. If you make mistakes—they are yours. Do not give your fruit, your ideas, your power, and your gifts away. Keep them and develop them for your best good. For when you are strong, mature, and nourished, you can then help your brothers and sisters by feeding them from your "fruit-full" bounty.

I cannot imagine what would have happened if Eve ate the fruit and did not give any to Adam. But knowing human nature, Adam would have probably taken some of the fruit anyway after seeing the effect on Eve. I cannot imagine a man living with a woman who knows more than he does . . . or then again, maybe I can.

It is a daily struggle to be our authentic self. There is a constant struggle to live our life in a unique way, unencumbered by the expectations of others. It is sometimes difficult to live a nonconforming life. It is not easy to walk another path, follow the beat of a different drum away from the messages of the majority voices. I remember when I was twelve and attending Goodwill Baptist Church. I was active in all the youth groups, especially the choir. All of us in the choir were between the ages of eleven and fifteen. Many of the adults had been asking us, "When are you going to join the church and get baptized?"

Some of us were reminded that after age twelve, our parents could not cover us spiritually; our sins were just that—ours.

One Sunday morning, after the pastor's sermon, the whole youth choir stood up and joined the church, except me. I was sitting there wondering, *What are they doing?* Maybe there had been a memo that I did not get, or a meeting I forgot to attend; whatever it was, I was out of the loop. I did not go up there, because I did not "feel" anything. I had no reason to join the church. I was doing everything possible in the church without membership, so what was the use? Of course, it seemed as if everyone was looking at me like the "Lone Sinner." I did not care; nothing had changed inside of me.

A year later, however, the youth group sponsored a revival. We had different preachers each night. On Thursday night, evangelist Mary E. Tilghman preached, and it was as if she was preaching directly to me. Ephesians 5:14–17: "Awake thou that sleepest, and arise from the dead and Christ shall give thee light. See then that ye walk circumspectly, not as fools, but as wise, redeeming the time, because the days are evil, wherefore be ye not unwise, but understanding what the will of the Lord is."

Her words pierced my heart. I felt a presence of God that I'd never experienced before. I felt that someone finally knew my hurts and pains, and someone loved me just as I was—God! I knew this in my head from Sunday school and reading the Bible, but at that moment I knew it in my heart and spirit. She did not "open the doors of the church," as we usually did at

Goodwill, but she extended an invitation for us to come and accept Jesus Christ as our personal Savior, and I did.

Just as everyone's conversion experience or moment of spiritual enlightenment is unique, so should every decision we make in life be unique. Are we that threatened when someone chooses a different path, calls God by another name, or colors outside the lines? Children have a wonderful way of doing things "their way" and not caring if you like it or not. Their way may take longer or be a bit more difficult to achieve, but the fulfillment is in knowing that it was their choice, their way, their accomplishment.

I encourage you to begin having an honest-to-God conversation with yourself about your reproductive health, your sexual well-being, and your core beliefs about yourself. Don't continue to follow the crowd; think for yourself. In my book *Oh God! A Black Woman's Guide to Sex and Spirituality*, I support women in their journey of discovery of their sexual-spiritual selves. In every situation, no matter what you have read or heard, ask yourself, *Is this what I want? Is this what is best for me?* After you have decided, then move forward into your life, more determined than ever to make yourself a priority on your list of things to do, not the footnote at the end of the day. You have the strength of your inner spirit to accomplish so many things, if only you would cooperate with your Inner Eve.

Always Apply Knowledge Immediately

The third lesson I see in this snake conspiracy is that we should always apply new knowledge immediately. When Eve ate the fruit from the tree of knowledge of good and evil, her eyes and mind were immediately opened to a higher intelligence. She had new information that heretofore was unavailable to anyone except God. It stands to reason that since she now had this new knowledge, she should have known that the snake was evil and had no good intentions toward her or Adam. I say, "Eve, kill the snake before he utterly destroys you!" Think about it with your new knowledge of good and evil. Why would this serpent spend his time enticing you to be disobedient to your Creator? What does it matter whether you eat the fruit or not? What's in it for him?

The main goal of this snake—and of snake-like people—is to destroy you and thus bring heartbreak to God. The serpent was jealous and could not stand the fact that God loved man so much that God created Adam and Eve in God's own image. He was racked with jealousy that they were created "a little lower than the angels." Adam and Eve had dominion over the snake and walked about freely without a care in the world, while he was subordinate and vulnerable to predators.

Immediately applied knowledge would also have informed them that a few hand-stitched fig leaves could not hide disobedience to God. God is all-knowing, all-powerful, and everywhere at the same time. Before we do things, God already knows what we're going to do. When God asked Adam and Eve, "Where are you?" it was not because God needed the information. Adam and Eve needed to realize and confess that they were not where they had been commanded by God to be—in God's will.

When I was a child my mother would come to me and my sister and ask us questions from time to time concerning something we'd done wrong. "Do you know what happened to my dishes?" "Have you seen my earrings?" "Where did you go after school today?" She did not ask these things because she needed information. She already knew what had happened. She was giving us the opportunity to confess and fall prostrate before her, begging for forgiveness for being inconsiderate and disobedient children. (I say this with tongue firmly in cheek.)

As with my mother, so it is with God. We read in James 4:17, "Therefore to him that knoweth to do good, and doeth it not, to him it is sin." It is not enough to know good and evil unless you are willing to apply your knowledge to your everyday choices and decisions. True knowledge is given from God. In Proverbs 4:7 it says, "Wisdom is the principal thing; therefore get wisdom: and with all thy getting get understanding." God's wisdom and understanding are accessible to us from within our spirits.

Some of us have become accustomed to seeking help outside ourselves. We believe that there is no way what we are looking for in life can be found within. Yet I'm beginning to think oth-

erwise. Spirit allows us to encounter people in our lives who
encourage us, test us, challenge us, and enlighten us. With
every year of life, new lessons come our way. Each year brings
its challenges, but also the strength to overcome them. There
are months full of hardships, but also the grace to make it
through. We have the treasure of our Inner Eve, God's Woman-
Spirit inside us, who is able to empower us beyond what we
could ever accomplish alone. In this life we will be "tested in
every way, but not crushed; perplexed, but not driven to despair; persecuted, but not forsaken; struck down, but not de-
stroyed" (II Corinthians 4:8–9).

To this day my favorite movie is *The Wizard of Oz*, with Judy
Garland playing Dorothy. Just like Dorothy, the Lion, the
Scarecrow, and the Tin Man, we have always had inside us
what we need to maneuver through this life. God has given
each of us courage, a heart, a mind, and a home. We need to
allow our Inner Eve greater power in our lives. If we would take
out the weeds of negativity that have grown up—by renewing
the Garden of our mind through trust, affirmations, self-love,
peace, hope, gentleness, kindness, patience, faith, and imagination—there are no limits to what we can achieve in our lives
and the lives of others. The Apostle Paul said it another way:
"Finally, beloved, whatever is true, whatever is honorable,
whatever is just, whatever is pure, whatever is pleasing, whatever is commendable, if there is any excellence and if there is
anything worthy of praise, think about these things" (Philippians 4:8).

Who am I? *I am Susan, God's original woman. I am a woman loved by God. I matter to God, and I matter to me.* It takes courage to live out your life in full expression of yourself. Don't live constantly seeking affirmation from others that you are valuable, important, wonderful, and worth loving. Affirm through your inner spirit that you are God's original woman, created in God's image. God knows you in your entirety, God loves you unconditionally, and you love yourself—that is enough.

INWARD REFLECTION

We must be willing to get rid of the life we've planned, so as to have the life that is waiting for us.

—JOSEPH CAMPBELL

Now that you've looked at Eve of Genesis, begin to reflect and consider how you can excavate your Inner Eve.

Most women have aspects of themselves that remain undiscovered. Like uncharted waters or uncrossed territories, we all have words never spoken and emotions we've never given expression to. We all have fears that linger only because we have not marshaled enough courage to dispel them. All of this can end right now, today. You will embark upon a new life. As they say in *Star Trek*, you will boldly go where you have never gone before—inward, toward your Inner Eve.

Begin to give expression to your Inner Eve. I want you to buy an artist's sketchbook and use it as a pictorial journal, a sort of collage with commentary. You can paste in pictures, write in the margins, and use colored markers. You can organize the pages in whatever manner suits you, but let the first section be "How I See My Eve." Get all your old magazines and cut out pictures that reflect how you feel on the inside, or that represent how you would like to look. I call this my dreamscape book. Create a section called "Me" that contains pictures reflecting how you feel, how you look, how you want to look. Are there things you want to change about yourself physically—hair, attire, contact lenses, body? How do you want to change inwardly? Paste words on this page's collage that represent change for you. Try words such as *courage, run, assertive, seduce, stop, flaunt, speak, more, live, passion,* and so forth.

Other sections of this dreamscape book can contain pictures and words that describe things you want in your home: wind chimes, a porch swing, an altar, an herb garden, a fitness room, a darkroom, a meditative sacred space, what have you. You may have always wanted a hope chest, but never purposefully sought to buy one. Find a picture of one you want and paste it in your dreamscape book. Maybe you want a chiming grandfather clock or a cherrywood sleigh bed. Maybe you've always wanted a player piano. Whatever is hidden beneath the surface of your conscious desires should be placed on the pages of your dreamscape.

These should be images of different types of things that please you. Pictures of places you wish to visit—Hawaii, Japan,

Africa, Vermont in winter, Los Angeles in summer, New Orleans at Mardi Gras. Don't forget to stop at newsstands or larger bookstores and pick up foreign magazines and international fashion magazines.

I suggest that you work on this at least two evenings a week. One day, just flip through magazines and cut out pictures. The other evening, paste, reflect, and write in the margins. You should spend time with your dreamscape book, and gradually begin to make some of these changes in your life. This is you giving hands and feet to your Inner Eve.

You can have a section on "Relationships," where you paste pictures of people who have been or are in your life now. What lessons did you learn from former relationships? What do you want in a relationship now? There is no right or wrong way to create this book. Have fun doing it, the way you did as a little girl with paper dolls. Doing this dreamscape book will offer you time to *play* with your Inner Eve, and discover her likes and dislikes. It would be funny to find out that she likes things that you've always liked, but never tried to acquire them.

Susanism

"It's never too late to have a happy childhood."

Chapter Two

THE PRAYERS
OF THE RIGHTEOUS

EVE POWERED UP!

I Samuel 1:1–20

Since September 11, 2001, fear and anxiety have gripped our country. Terror is not just global, though; it happens in our homes as well. More incidents of mothers killing their children are occurring. Andrea Yates, a Texas mother, drowned her five children in the bathtub; Susan Smith in South Carolina strapped her two babies into the car and rolled it into a lake; and most recently Deanna Laney, of Texas, bludgeoned her two sons to death because she believed God commanded it. It's praying time. Many have had their faith tested and trust betrayed because of the scandals involving the Catholic Church. It's praying time.

In James 5:13, the Bible asks the question, "Is there any among you suffering? Then let them pray." Let's look at a woman by the name of Hannah who did just that when faced with a crisis. In the book of I Samuel, chapter 1, we find a Jewish man, Elkanah, who had two wives: Peninnah, who bore him many sons and daughters, and Hannah, who was barren.

In a culture where a woman's worth was measured by the fruit of her womb, Hannah was barren, and she desperately wanted to have a child. After exhausting all human efforts, she sought God through prayer—and her prayers were answered.

Leading up to the Day of Atonement, the people of Hannah's day would fast and prepare themselves to confess their sins to God, but after the sacrifices had been made, a great banquet was held and all the people would make merry because God had spared their lives another year. Portions of the food were given to each wife according to the number of children she bore her husband. Well, Peninnah's plate was supersized, while poor Hannah had to settle for a Happy Meal. And Peninnah would ridicule Hannah because she had no children to please Elkanah. It seemed that every year when they went to Shiloh, Peninnah's portion increased while Hannah was reminded of her failure.

Yet I'm sure there were many others like Hannah, who came to Shiloh year after year just as burdened when they left as when they arrived. Hannah sat in the Outer Court of the temple, called the Court of Women, with the other women, as well as children and slaves, while the men worshiped in the Inner Court, the Court of Israel, near the altar of God. Hannah sat through the service listening to the men pray the same prayers she'd heard her grandfather, father, brothers, and husband pray all her life. "Praised be God that He has not created me a Gentile; praised be God that He has not created me a woman; praised be God that He has not created me an ignorant man." She listened as confessions of sins were made, and she listened

to the priest's annual Day of Atonement message, "Please Be
Patient with Me, Yahweh's Not Through with Me Yet."

Hannah was so distracted. Here she was sitting in the Outer
Court, unable to hear the entire message. She would wipe her
brow with her handkerchief, fan herself with palm leaves, and
could not help but notice a little boy sweetly sleeping on his
mother's lap. She turned her head and absentmindedly
watched another woman breast-feed her newborn girl. Hannah
ached. She was not allowed in the Inner Court of the temple
with the men, and she felt out of place in the Outer Court with
the women. Why did she come to Shiloh anyway?

After worship, as everyone was preparing for the feast, Hannah could not help but notice how some of the women were
glancing at her out of the corner of their eyes. She overheard
some of them saying, "I wonder, what sin did she commit that
God made her barren?" Another group would be gathered
around Peninnah as she sowed seeds of deceit, telling lies about
how Hannah was one of those liberated women who really
didn't want children anyway. You know they believed Peninnah because she lived in the same house with Hannah.

Some of the women felt sorry for Hannah and would give
her advice. The older women would tell her, "Chile, when I
was your age and just got married, I couldn't get pregnant, either. I tell you what to do, go out in the field and gather leaves
from a mandrake plant and make some tea. Drink this tea three
times a day and before you know it you'll have some little baby
feet running around your home."

The younger women would come to Hannah and say, "Sistergirl, women don't just get pregnant when they want to—timing is important. You make sure Elkanah is in your tent and not Peninnah's the night of the new moon, and you'll be knitting baby booties in no time." But year after year, full of mandrake tea and twelve new moons later, Hannah would come to Shiloh just as burdened and barren as the years before.

Then one year, something happened on her visit to Shiloh: Something changed inside Hannah. I can't imagine what it was, but she stopped having her pity party and decided to pray about her situation. Maybe it was while listening to the men thank God for not creating them women that Hannah began to praise God for creating her a woman and not a man. Maybe Hannah saw one of the women brushing her daughter's hair and remembered the closeness and love of her own mother's nurturing when she was a child. Hannah wanted more than ever to experience motherhood. The transformation of her spirit may have come while she watched the little girls laugh and play patty-cake games, and Hannah remembered her childhood as their singsong voices drifted through the Mediterranean air: "Eney, meany, jip-sa-line, ooh-ah-ah-ma-liene, atchie, catchie, Liberace I love you!"

I'm not sure what it was, but while sitting at the Day of Atonement banquet that year Hannah began to change. She started to think differently about what prayer really did in the lives of her people. It was their prayers and petitions before God that saved their lives another year. Prayer was powerful, and it couldn't get any better than here where the tabernacle of

God stood. Prayer wasn't just some spiritual bookends tacked onto the beginning and end of festive occasions. Prayer was a way of telling God what was in a person's heart—the burdens and the blessings.

Elkanah noticed that Hannah seemed distracted as she fidgeted with her napkin, and he asked her, "Hannah, what's wrong?" Hannah, looking in her empty plate, replied thoughtfully, "I only get one portion of meat at this banquet each year because I have no children." Elkanah, not understanding what was going on inside Hannah's spirit, tried to comfort her and patted her hand, saying, "There, there, Hannah, am I not more to you than ten sons?" Hannah rose up from the table and ran out of the banquet toward the temple. Elkanah started to go after her, but Peninnah restrained him, saying, "Let her go. Give your attention to your children and their mother."

Hannah ran to the temple. Her tears filled her eyes so that she did not see Eli, the priest, as she ran past him. She went into the Court of Women and fell on her knees, weeping bitterly. There were not words in the Hebrew language to express the pain and anguish Hannah felt as she prayed. She prayed to God that if God would grant her a son, she would give the boy back to God in the service of the temple. Can't you just see her praying, saying, "God, you blessed Sarah with a son—bless me. God, you blessed Rebecca with a son—bless me. God, you blessed Rachel with a son—bless me. God, you did it for Samson's mother—God, do it for me!"

There is something about human nature—we do not get serious with God until we are at the end of our rope. We run to God after we've tried everybody else's remedy, listened to everyone's advice, or tried all the other solutions. Oh yes, we pray all the time, but many of us don't pray with our spirit until our spirit is in turmoil. Many others don't pray until we are driven to our knees by the circumstances of life. Some would ask, like Peninnah's friends, "What sin did Hannah commit that God made her barren? What awful thing did she do in her youth that she is so troubled now?" Similar questions were posed to Jesus by his disciples one day. Jesus and his disciples encountered a man who was blind from birth. The disciples asked, "Master, who did sin, this man, or his parents that he was born blind?" Jesus answered, "Neither hath this man sinned, nor his parents; but that the words of God might be made manifest in him," and Jesus healed the man that moment (John 9:1–3). When we have reached our limits, God is just approaching God's possibilities. When we hit rock bottom, that's when we discover that there is a Rock higher than us.

Hannah was praying in her spirit. Her mouth was moving, and the sounds that emanated from her lips did not seem to make sense. Her words were inaudible to the human ear, but the divine ear of God understood every syllable. In her weakness, God's Spirit was interceding on Hannah's behalf in prayer. As she prayed, Eli stood in the shadows watching. He thought Hannah had had too much to drink at the banquet. He came to her and said, "Hannah, wife of Elkanah, it is a shame for a woman like you to be in the temple drunk! Haven't you had enough to drink for one festival? Put your wine away."

Eli didn't understand what was going on in Hannah's heart. He simply saw a woman mumbling to herself, lying all on the floor and everything. Nobody came to the temple at Shiloh just to sit and pray! But Hannah stood up and said, "I'm not a drunk woman, I'm a troubled woman who needs to hear from God. I poured out my soul to the Lord, asking God to hear my prayers." Eli was so impressed that someone had come to the temple to do some serious praying that he said, "Go in peace, and may God answer your prayer."

Hannah went back to the banquet and ate, but she didn't return looking depressed; her whole countenance was changed. I can imagine that when she walked back to the table where Elkanah and Peninnah were sitting, Hannah said, "Peninnah, would you be a dear and pour me a glass of punch, please?" Peninnah probably snidely replied, "Are you sure you don't want some mandrake tea for your condition?" And Hannah said, "I don't need mandrake tea, I've got all I need—a good husband and a greater God."

The next day they left Shiloh and went back home. Hannah started acting differently because she had prayed in faith and said "Amen," which means "It is so." Hannah believed that God would do God's part if she did hers. Elkanah was working in the fields, and when he came home that evening, I can see Hannah in preparation mode for a romantic evening. I can imagine Hannah as she prepared her bath and dropped rose petals in the water. She fixed Elkanah's favorite meal and put on that sexy black dress he brought back from his trip to Gibeah. Peninnah was in her quarters and could hear the music coming from Hannah's room—it sounded like Teddy Pendergrass singing "Turn Off the Lights." The Bible said, "Elkanah *knew* [that's the biblical term for sexual relations] Hannah his wife, and the Lord remembered her and in due time Hannah conceived and bore a son, and she called his name Samuel. After Samuel was born, Hannah weaned him and took him to the Temple in Shiloh and praised God in song for answering her prayer."

Isn't it odd that when Hannah displayed a greater fervor with her prayer life, the priest thought she must be drunk? The same may happen when you decide to transform your religious life from traditional expressions to fervent spiritual disciplines of meditation, personal devotion, fasting, and prayer. As soon as you stop being "religious"—looking and acting the way religious folks are supposed to look and act—the religious folks start talking about you. Our religious traditions bring us only so far along the way in our spiritual growth and maturity, but the continuous, deliberate practice of spiritual principles such as prayer and meditation empowers us to accomplish the greater things in life.

For you see, there is a difference between being religious and being spiritual. It is because of my spirituality—which is the Spirit of God present within my human spirit, guiding and controlling my life—that I choose to live out my spiritual life in a religious fashion, meaning in a church on Sunday, with stained-glass windows, a pipe organ, and an order of worship that includes preludes, introits, processionals, invocations, prayer and praise teams, announcements, hymnbooks, bulletins, choir robes, and ushers. That's my religious way of expressing my spirituality. But sometimes I choose to live out my spirituality in the mountains, wearing jeans, a T-shirt, and sandals. The river provides the prelude, and the birds sing in chorus. The scripture is read by the landscape, for everywhere I look, I see God. "The Earth is the Lord's and the fullness thereof, the world and they that dwell therein" (Psalms 24:1).

Jesus' commitment to prayer is seen early in the morning and late at night. The Gospel of Mark 1:35 says, "And in the morning, a great while before day, he rose and went out to a lonely place, and there he prayed." Luke 6:12 says, "And it came to pass in those days, that he went out into a mountain to pray, and continued all night in prayer to God." If Jesus, being God in human form, found prayer to be a necessary ingredient in His life, how can we neglect so great a practice?

David's dedication to prayer is seen in Psalms 63:1—"Early will I seek Thee." It is prayer that ushers us into the presence of God and opens the path to communion with the Almighty.

No one ever begins a life of prayer as a spiritual giant. God always meets us where we are and slowly moves us along into deeper things. Youths who run track and field for their high school teams do not suddenly decide to enter the Olympics; they train and grow stronger and later are able to compete in the great event. Likewise our prayer lives. We begin where we are, practicing the principles of our prayer, and one day we will find ourselves doing the greater things in life.

Sisters, take your burdens to the Lord and leave them there! As the hymn of the church says:

> *What a friend we have in Jesus,*
> *All our sins and griefs to bear*
> *What a privilege to carry,*
> *Everything to God in prayer.*
> *Oh what peace we often forfeit,*
> *Oh what needless pain we bear,*
> *All because we do not carry*
> *Everything to God in prayer.*

Believe the Word of God when it says, Is there any among you suffering? Let them pray. . . . The prayers of the righteous availeth much; Trust in the Lord with all thine heart and lean not unto thine own understanding, in all thy ways acknowledge God and God shall direct thy paths; Ask and it shall be given you, seek and ye shall find, knock, and it shall be opened unto you; for everyone that asketh, receiveth; and she that seeketh findeth; and to him that knocketh, it shall be opened" (James 5:13 and 5:16; Proverbs 3:5; Matthew 7:7–8).

INWARD REFLECTION

Nothing is more surprising than the rise of the new within ourselves.

—PAUL TILLICH

Like Hannah, women face challenges all through life.
As women of faith, we believe in the power of prayer.
Let's reflect and consider how to strengthen
our Inner Eve through prayer.

In this chapter I talked about prayer. I would like you to consider the following questions:

⁓ What areas in your life do you want to develop through prayer?

⁓ What do you need from God to nurture your Inner Eve?

⁓ Have you ever experienced an "inner yes" in regard to praying for a particular concern? If so, what effect did it have on your prayer life?

I'd like you to reflect on these scriptures, thinking about how they inform your prayers:

If you abide in me, and my words abide in you, ask for whatever you wish, and it will be done for you.

JOHN 15:7

You ask and do not receive, because you ask wrongly, in order to spend what you get on your pleasures.

JAMES 4:3

And finally, add your words to this prayer list for your Inner Eve: *Dear God . . .*

❧ *Help me think clearly in all my situations.*

❧ *Help me stay open and receptive.*

❧ *Help me make a commitment and follow through.*

❧ *Teach me to be patient and generous with myself and others.*

❧ *Help me be a better woman, wife, mother, and friend.*

❧ *Keep me focused on my future goals.*

❧ *Help me love and adore my body.*

❧ *Honor me with your presence, love, and serenity.*

Susanism

"Always pray for greater things."

Chapter Three

THE HANDS OF A WOMAN

EVE ACTING UP!

Judges 4:1–21

Bill Withers recorded the song "Grandma's Hands" about his grandmother and what he remembered about her hands. Those closest to us can distinguish the touch of our hands from that of a stranger. In the Bible, Isaac was old and feeble, and ready to bless either his son Esau or his son Jacob with his blessing of inheritance. His wife, Rebecca, helped her son Jacob fool Isaac by covering Jacob's hands with hair, for Esau was hairy and Jacob was not. But listen to the words of old and feeble Isaac: "Jacob went near unto Isaac his father; and he felt him, and said, the voice is Jacob's voice, but the hands are the hands of Esau" (Genesis 27:22). What do people know about you by your hands? Not just by how they look and feel, but by what they do.

Let's look at how God can save a people through women and their hands. During the period of the Judges, Israel was not an established nation. It had no king. Moses led the Israelites out of slavery in Egypt. After Moses' death on Mount Pisgah, Joshua led them into the Promised Land—Canaan.

The land was full of various nations—the Philistines, the Canaanites, the Midianites, the Ammonites, the Moabites, the Sidonites, and the Hivites. Each nation had its own gods that its people worshiped. But the Israelites were commanded to worship only their God—Jehovah. Under Joshua's leadership, the people were faithful to God, but after Joshua died they became idolatrous and bowed down before strange gods. According to Judges 17:6, "Every man did that which was right in his own eyes." The Lord was no longer "King in Israel." The tribes were divided; the people were mixing with the heathen nations; and it was necessary for God to chasten the people.

Their lives became a cycle of sin, invasion, and deliverance for several years. The Israelites would forsake God, then be enslaved by the people whose gods they worshiped; they would cry to the Lord in repentance for their sins, and God would raise up a judge to deliver them.

These judges were first of all deliverers, and then administrators of justice who settled disputes and concerns between individuals. The chief military judges were Othniel, Ehud, Deborah, Gideon, Jephtha, and Samson, and there were seven minor judges. These thirteen judges were each raised up by God to defeat a particular enemy and give the people rest. They were not national leaders; rather, they were local leaders who delivered the people from various oppressors.

In the fourth chapter of Judges, we find our Inner Eve in action, as seen in the lives of two women—Deborah, a judge, and Jael, a housewife. Deborah was a prophetess and wife of Lappidoth. God anointed her to serve as a judge in Mount Ephraim, where she sat under a palm tree and counseled the people. For twenty years the Israelites were oppressed by the cruel aggressor Sisera, the general of the Canaanite army. Deborah sent for Barak, the general of the Israelite army, and said, "The Lord, the God of Israel, commands you 'Go, take position at Mount Tabor, bringing 10,000 from the tribe of Naphtali and the tribe of Zebulun. I will draw out Sisera, the general of Jabin's army, to meet you by the Wadi Kishon with his chariots and his troops; and I will give him into your hand.' " Barak replied, "If you will go with me, I will go; but if you will not go with me, I will not go." She said, "I will surely go with you; nevertheless, the road on which you are going will not lead to your glory, for the Lord will sell Sisera into the hand of a woman."

So the Bible says Deborah got up and went with Barak. Can you imagine that? Here was a man, a general of the Israeli army, saying he would not obey God's command and go into battle unless Deborah, a woman, went with him. Now, as a Womanist I got nothing but mad love for the brother to recognize the anointing of God on Deborah, and respect her leadership enough to want her with him in battle. In the day, culture, and time that this happened, however, it was unheard of for a man to defer to a woman before doing anything—especially a warrior like Barak.

What we have here is a new paradigm of male-female relationships—a reversal of traditional gender roles. But what do you do with a "Deborah woman" and a "Barak man"? Here we have a woman with courage enough to lead, and a man with confidence enough to ask a woman to accompany him in a major undertaking—war. Can you imagine what the troops thought? "What is Deborah doing leading us into battle? Shouldn't she be back under her palm tree working on a Bible lesson, or home fixing Lappidoth's dinner?" Whatever was said, we know that General Barak was wise enough to know that he did not want to go into battle without God's anointed leader by his side.

As women we have often found ourselves just waiting for our own inner consent to move out, speak up, act up, and show up. Our Inner Eve is waiting to express herself in a new dimension, and sometimes in a nontraditional role, but a much-needed and God-ordained role.

Another example of this involves the sisters Mary and Martha, and their encounter with Jesus in Bethany. Jesus had stopped by his friends' home in Bethany, as he often did, for comfort and relaxation. Martha was in the kitchen cooking dinner and fussing about. Mary was in the family room sitting with Jesus as he talked with her about the law and the prophets. Martha scolded Mary for sitting down while she was busy in the kitchen and wanted Jesus to do something about it: " 'Lord, do you not care that my sister has left me to do all the work by myself? Tell her then to help me.' But the Lord answered her, 'Martha, Martha, you are worried and distracted by many things; there is need of only one thing. Mary has chosen the better part, which will not be taken away from her' " (Luke 10:40–42).

There's a little Mary and a little Martha in all of us. There's the woman who lives out the traditional, expected female role, and there is the part of us that is ready and able to move in another realm at any moment. Some sisters are the reverse. Folks around such a woman are used to seeing her in nontraditional roles, but surprised to see her in the "domestic" realm. She owns her own company, is the founding CEO of her own corporation. She's the senior pastor of the church. She's the senator, the Supreme Court justice, the dean of the medical school, and she is a wife (or single mother, or loving partner) and an extraordinary cook. Sometimes women may find themselves in a role that is not seen as traditional by their culture or family, but if God calls you to a work, God will prepare you for it.

In the story of Deborah and Barak leading the Israelite army into battle against General Sisera and the Canaanites, there's a subplot that eventually overshadows even Deborah's presence in battle. There was a woman named Jael. She was not a prophetess or a judge. She was a housewife, the spouse of Heber, a Kenite. King Jabin of Canaan enjoyed a peaceful relationship with the Kenites. So in the heat of the battle, when Barak and Deborah were gaining the victory over all of Sisera's chariots and all his men were killed by the sword, Sisera fled for his life toward the dwellings of the Kenites.

Jael was probably outside the tent beating sand off one of the rugs. She saw Sisera running and called out to him, "Turn in my lord, turn in to me and fear not." She covered him with a rug. Then he asked her for something to drink. She gave him a drink and covered him again. He asked her to stand outside the tent and, if anyone asked whether she'd seen him, say "No." He picked up no threat from this housewife. She was not a prophetess, she was not a leader, and she was not a warrior. So, feeling secure, Sisera fell asleep. It was then that Jael took a nail of the tent and hammered it into Sisera's forehead and killed him, thus fulfilling Deborah's prophecy that the general would be delivered into the hands of a woman.

Now, this story may seem a bit gruesome to some, but this was war. Imagine yourself as a slave during the Civil War, when you spot the most brutal oppressor—who beat your son with the lash and whip, sold your children away, raped your sisters, and killed your husband—fleeing from Yankee troops. He comes to your slave quarters and hides under the rug, asking you to distract anyone who might come looking for him, then falls asleep. What would you do?

Instead of Sisera being killed by Barak's sword, he was killed by Jael and what she had in her hands. The Inner Eve within Jael told her she was not just a housewife. Eve informed her that there was more to her day than beating the rugs, milking the goats, and cooking for Heber. This was the day for her Inner Eve to show up and show out. What Jael did saved the lives of the Israelites. If Sisera had survived, he would have recruited more troops and built more chariots and oppressed more men, women, and children. Jael's Inner Eve put a stop to that.

Jael did three things that we can apply to ourselves, helping us move from where we are to where God is calling us to be.

She started where she was, she used what she had, and she did what she could. Jael did not get on a horse and ride out to Mount Tabor, where the battle was being fought. She stayed in the plains of Zaanaim by Kedesh and took care of her tent. She started where she was.

Sometimes God needs us right where we are. Do you work on a college or university campus? God needs you there. Do you work in a public school? God needs you there. Do you live in a troubled neighborhood? God needs you there. God needs Spirit-motivated women in Durham, Chicago, Houston, New York, Detroit, Oakland, DC, Sumter, and Atlanta. I cannot count the number of sisters I've had conversations with who feel that they need to do something, so they think about moving somewhere new.

Now, let's be clear: If where you are geographically poses a threat to your life or well-being—move! If where you are does not afford you freedom from oppression—move right now. If you know, that you know, that you know, sho'nuff that God is calling you to move—get going! But if that is not the case, stand still and see what God would have you do right where you are. Don't move geographically; move spiritually. Begin an inward journey to see and hear what God is saying to your Inner Eve. What does Spirit say to you in devotion and prayer? Seek God's face; be attuned to God's voice; look for God's hand. And if you don't see God's hand right away, look for God's fingerprints.

We can only find satisfaction and fulfillment in life doing

the will of God, where God has called us to work. You may think you got your job because of your impressive résumé, or your communication skills, or your tight network of friends. This may be partially true, but as Christians, "We know that all things work together for the good, to them that love God and are called according to God's purpose" (Romans 8:28). Success occurs when opportunity meets preparation. Get prepared; your opportunity is coming to you right where you are.

Jael also used what she had—a tent nail and a hammer. She did not go to the army boot camp to get trained as an archer or sword fighter; she used what she had. What do you have to use to strike a mighty blow for someone in this world? She used what she had; what do you have that God can use? I can hear some of you saying, "All I got is my little apartment, a 1997 Honda, and a fixed income that will not move." That may be true, but you also have treasure and resources that God can use. We serve a God "who is able to do exceedingly, abundantly above anything we can ask, think or imagine, according to the power that worketh in us" (Ephesians 3:20). You don't have to look far to find something that God can use. Let's call a few witnesses who can testify to God's use of what they had.

What do you have, David? David says, "I was a shepherd boy, tending my family's sheep. I was skilled in defending the flock against the attack of wild animals. I killed a bear one day with my slingshot. One day I brought food to my brothers who fought in our nation's army against the Philistines. There was a giant of a man named Goliath who threatened them and cursed our God. I was determined to stand up to him. All I had was my slingshot and five smooth stones from the riverbed. God was with me, and I felt the hand of God on my hand and that slingshot. The rock struck the giant in the temple and he fell dead to the ground."

"I'd like to testify. I'm Mary McLeod Bethune. I'm a Negro woman born to former slaves in Maysville, South Carolina. I had seventeen brothers and sisters. Early in life I discovered that education was a powerful road to freedom for the Negro people, especially the women. In 1904 I lived in Daytona, Florida. I had $1.50 in my hands. With this little bit of money, I began a school with just five pupils. I called it the Daytona Literary and Industrial School for Training Negro Girls. With God's help, and my gifts as a teacher and administrator, I expanded the school to a high school, then a junior college, and finally it became Bethune-Cookman College."

Not only did Jael start where she was, and use what she had—Jael did what she could, too. What can you do, sisters? Women today have more opportunity and resources than at any other time in our history. What can you do? I think about women who've had so much working against them, and so few resources, but their lives have been an inspiration to so many and a testimony to their Inner Eve.

Chief Wilma Mankiller is a powerful visionary and the first woman principal chief of the Cherokee Nation. She is responsible for 139,000 people and a $69 million budget. Born in 1945 on a farm in Oklahoma, she and her ten siblings were

moved to San Francisco by the Bureau of Indian Affairs because of a drought in the 1950s. Wilma graduated from high
school and began advanced studies at San Francisco State University. She married, traveled to South America and Europe,
gave birth to two daughters, and returned to the San Francisco
area. Education helped her to better understand the plight
of her people and equipped her to better serve Native Ameri-
cans. Her concern for Native American issues was ignited in
1969 when a group of university students occupied Alcatraz
Island in order to attract attention to the issues affecting
their tribes. Shortly afterward, she began working in preschool
and adult education programs in the Pit River Tribe of California.

Wilma divorced her husband of eleven years when their
views of her role diverged. In 1975 she returned to Oklahoma
with her daughters. Settling near Tahlequah, the national
headquarters of the Cherokee Nation of Oklahoma, she immediately began helping her people by procuring grants enabling
them to launch critical rural programs. In 1983 she ran for
deputy chief, and in 1985 Mankiller became principal chief, a
position she holds today. Mankiller has brought about important strides for the Cherokee, including improved health care,
education, utilities management, and tribal government. Plans
call for attracting higher-paying industry to the area, improv-
ing adult literacy, supporting women returning to school, and
more. Mankiller also lives in the larger world, active in civil
rights matters, lobbying the federal government, and support-

ing women's activities and issues. She says: "Prior to my election, young Cherokee girls would never have thought that they might grow up and become chief."

It is so important to listen to the voice of God speaking from within. When we nurture ourselves spiritually and are sometimes called upon to go the extra mile for some cause or someone, God will honor our spirited devotion and sacrifice. You will never know whose life will be transformed by your example of love and devotion.

There are a few women who have been my inspiration in life. Lillian Newman, my mother, is on the top of my list. She worked more than one job to make sure my sister, Connie, and I had what we needed and a lot of what we wanted. Unfortunately, my father was plagued by alcoholism. The eagle would fly on Friday, and Daddy would come home with his paycheck cashed. He'd get dressed up and go out with his friends. We would not see him again until sometime Sunday. He'd come home despondent and broke.

Momma would work longer hours to make ends meet. She was a licensed cosmetologist for years back home in Danville, Virginia. After moving to DC, Momma worked as a manicurist at Ewell's Barbershop in downtown Washington. Before the riots of 1968, the New York Avenue and F Street area of downtown DC was thriving with businesses, theaters, and activity. Well-to-do white and black businessmen came to Ewell's Barbershop to get their hair cut and nails manicured. I used to love coming downtown on a Saturday with Connie to watch

Momma buff and manicure nails. We would walk down the aisle of chairs, and the men would smile and tell us how proud Momma was of us and how smart we were. They'd give us Kennedy fifty-cent coins and dollar bills.

We were never hungry or without good clothes to wear, and no one knew what went on behind our closed doors. My father's alcoholism sometimes rendered him depressed, other times violent. Through it all, Momma made a life for us. Her one day off work was Monday. She would get home from work Sunday evenings around five o'clock and take us out to the movies, or we'd just ride the bus to downtown DC and look in the windows of the Woodward and Lothrop. She would take us to the Howard Johnson's restaurant and we'd order a HoJo Orange Freeze and practice our table manners.

When we were in junior high school, Momma went to college and began working in DC public schools as an educational aide. We were so proud of her hard work and sacrifice. She started where she was, used what she had, and did what she could.

Dr. Martin Luther King Jr. once said, "If a man is called to be a street sweeper, he should sweep streets as Michelangelo painted or Beethoven composed music, or Shakespeare wrote poetry. He should sweep streets so well that all of the host of heaven and earth will pause to say, 'Here is a great street sweeper who did his job well.'"

The Bible encourages us to use all our resources and become who we can and do what we can. "Beloved now we are the children of God and it doth not yet appear what we shall be, for eyes have not seen nor ear heard, neither has it entered our hearts the things that God has prepared for those who love him" (I John 3:2, I Corinthians 2:9).

INWARD REFLECTION

Everyone is necessarily the hero of his own life story.

—JOHN BARTH

We have looked at women whose lives have influenced so many. Let's reflect and consider how our God-inspired minds can guide our Inner Eve.

When difficulties arise—and they will—our Inner Eve is ready to help us. It is not just what happens to us that shapes who we become, but also what happens *in* us that makes the difference between who becomes a heroine and who remains a victim. No matter how you are treated, maintain a sense of yourself—apart from who others say you are. Assess the past; decide how to act in the present; and make plans for your future.

Circumstances will occur not of our own choosing, but we can approach them with the *attitude* that our choices matter, until we really believe they do. No matter what Spirit brings into your day, always approach it from your Inner Eve by:

🙢 Assessing what you can do.

🙢 Assessing what you will do.

❧ Behaving in ways consistent with your values and feelings—you must act as the heroine of your own life.

Susanism

"*Start where you are, use what you have,
and do what you can.*"

Chapter Four

THIS IS NOT A TIME
FOR SILENCE

EVE SPEAKING UP!

I Corinthians 14:33–35

When I was a first-year seminarian at the Howard University Divinity School, New Testament professor Dr. Thomas Hoyt (now Bishop Hoyt) was always challenging our thoughts and theology, challenging us to not be afraid to examine closely beliefs that we held dear to our hearts about God and how God deals with us in our everyday lives. Whenever we would examine the writings of the Old Testament laws and compare the teachings of the prophets to the teachings and lifestyle of Jesus, we would see clearly that Jesus' way of being and doing the will of God was not the traditional or customary way at that time. Dr. Hoyt used to quote from a hymn, "Once to Every Man and Nation": "New occasions teach new duties, time makes ancient truths uncouth." It took me a while to understand this, but I've come to interpret it as: *Always be ready for God to do a new thing, even when it seems impossible, for with God all things are possible.*

Ecclesiastes 3 teaches, "There is a season and a time to every purpose under the heaven . . . a time to keep silence, and a time to speak." Sisters, this is not a time to be silent!

In our text we read from a letter the Apostle Paul wrote to the Christians in the church at Corinth. He received a letter from a sister of the church, complaining about the many problems they were experiencing. You think churches today have problems, look with me at this early church in Corinth. There were cliques or factions in the church. They were not unified. Some hung together and thought they had a special spiritual knowledge because they were baptized by Apollos; others allied themselves with Paul. Some were baptized by Peter, and some identified solely with Jesus Christ. Paul wrote to the church in Corinth that it was not important who baptized you, only that you believed and were baptized into the body of Christ.

Then there was this little problem of incest in one of the families of the church. A young man was having an affair with a woman who was not his mother, but was his father's wife, and the church folks knew about it and did nothing. Christians were suing other Christians in court. Things were a mess, and then came the big issue—sex and marriage, what to do, and what not to do. Corinth was a seaport between Asia and Italy, and the newest fads and kinkiest lifestyles came to town. The latest dances started in Corinth; the strangest hairstyles were designed in Corinth. The most seductive clothing worn by people of that day was most likely made in Corinth.

So here Paul had a church full of "baby" Christians, some

who had in the past worshiped pagan gods at the temple of Aphrodite, where they participated in sexual rituals with temple prostitutes, and some who were Jews who now accepted Jesus Christ as the Messiah—a group of people with different upbringings and backgrounds. But whether these men were former Greek worshipers of Aphrodite or messianic Jews, they all viewed women in a dim light.

Picture this: For one group of men, women were sex objects in their worship; for the other group, women sat in the Outer Court with the slaves and children and were not seen or heard. Only the men read from the Torah and prayed to God. Only the male priest could administer the prayers behind the Holy of Holies. So now the Jewish women who had become followers of Jesus Christ, who no longer worshiped in the segregated temples but who sat with men in this new church at Corinth, were in a strange new social setting.

They worshiped in the large rooms of someone's home. Women sat on one side of the room, and the men on the opposite. Even though their religious traditions changed because they now worshiped Jesus Christ as the Messiah of the Jews, these men and women were still Jews by culture and followed the strict traditions and customs regarding women and men associating in public. Men were not permitted to speak to women in public—not even to their own wives. It was seen as beneath a man to speak to a woman. Many forget that the first Christians of the early church were Jews, and still lived their lives according to the instructions of the Talmud.

Little boys were instructed in the ways of the Jews, studying the law and prophets with a rabbi. When a boy reached the age of twelve, he had a bar mitzvah and read from the Torah for the first time in the Council of Men, in the Inner Court of the Sabbath worship. After their bar mitzvah, they no longer sat in the Outer Court with the women, slaves, and small children—they joined the men.

Women were not allowed to read the Torah, or to learn the ways of God or the words of the Prophets. Rabbinic teachings from the Mishnah, Sotah 3:4, say, "Rather should the words of the Torah be burned than entrusted to a woman. Whoever teaches his daughter the Torah is like one who teaches her obscenity." The Word of God was only for men.

Paul, a Jewish man, proud of his heritage, described himself in his letter to the Philippians 3:5: "Circumcised the eighth day, of the stock of Israel, of the tribe of Benjamin, a Hebrew of Hebrews; as touching the law, a Pharisee." In this Greek-influenced world, the Pharisees opposed the Hellenistic culture and adhered strictly to the Mosaic institution, demanding the same of all Jews. So here was Paul, who'd experienced a dramatic conversion on the Damascus Road from a strict Pharisee to a follower of Jesus Christ. This man was the founding pastor of the flavorful church in Corinth and went on to plant other churches.

Paul would start a church and move on to other cities, leaving preachers and teachers such as Apollos, Cephas, and others to lead the people. These men would preach about Jesus, who is the Christ, the One who was prophesied to come and make a highway through the desert. The One whom Isaiah said would hold the government upon His shoulders. The One whom Ezekiel said was a wheel in the middle of a wheel. The One whom Jeremiah said would be David's Righteous Branch, a king who would reign and prosper, and execute judgment and justice in the earth, the Lord of Righteousness.

Throughout these fiery sermons and teachings, the women would not understand everything that was being said, because they were never given the opportunity to study the prophets or the law and did not understand all the references to scripture that the men grew up learning. So Salome would get up and cross the room to ask her husband, Levi, "What did Apollos mean when he said, 'So and so or such and such'?" Then she would return to her seat back across the aisle. About ten minutes later, Judith would raise her finger and tiptoe around to the back of the room to ask her brother Stephen, "What did Apollos mean when he said 'The fathers have sinned and the children's teeth are set on edge'?" Women were going back and forth across the room during the entire service, trying to get some clarity about the sermon being preached or lesson being taught. All this activity was of course causing disorder and confusion in the worship.

You know how annoying it is when you're trying to enjoy the worship service or focus on the sermon and people are squeezing past you to go to the bathroom, or make a phone call, or just walk in and out to be seen. Well, this was the straw that broke the proverbial camel's back. Some of those folks "which are of the house of Chloe" wrote the Apostle Paul a long letter cataloging all these problems (I Corinthians 1:11) and seeking his counsel concerning these "contentions." Paul tried to address them all from his perspective as a Jewish man, steeped in Jewish customs, laws, and traditions.

Paul answered, "God is not the author of confusion, but of peace, as in all churches of the saints. Let your women keep silent in the churches; for it is not permitted unto them to speak but they are commanded to be under obedience as also saith the law. And if they will learn anything, let them ask their husbands at home: for it is a shame for women to speak in the church."

Now, Paul had written this long letter (fifteen chapters) to the church offering advice about uniting the divided groups, not taking each other to court, dealing with the incest and irresponsible sexuality in their lives, marriage and celibacy, gifts of the Spirit, the greatest gift of love, and here, at the end of his catalog of comments and advice, Paul must simply have been weary from all these church problems and quickly said, in essence, *God is not the author of confusion. Just tell the women to keep quiet during worship. Remind them that according to the law, they're supposed to be seen and not heard anyway!*

We all know you should not try to counsel or give advice when you're exhausted. Examine his advice with me. First, he says they are "not permitted to speak by the law." I'll come back to that, but then he says, "If they are to learn anything"—as if he hardly thought this possible, since women were seen as given to idle gossip and myths. Women's wisdom and intuition have historically been called "old wives' tales." But "if they are to learn, let them ask their husbands at home."

Well, all you single women can hang it up. Paul assumes that all good church women have a husband. And if you have a husband, he'll be home when you get there. And if he is at home when you get there, he is ready to have Bible study with you and discuss the sermon or the lesson. I don't know about your house, but after church on most Sundays, brothers I know don't want to have Bible study, or discuss the sermon. Usually it is kick-off time, tip-off time, tee-off time, or eat-and-sleep time. So, Paul, what are the single women or those whose men are preoccupied supposed to do?

As I mentioned, Paul said the women are not "permitted by law to speak." Was this Paul quoting from the law? He said in Romans 10, "For Christ is the end of the law for righteousness to everyone that believeth." (See also Romans 6:14; 7:4–6; and 8:1–4.)

Well, if Christ is the end of the law, and we are under grace, why was Paul dragging up those dusty old law books? It's interesting how folks can go back to the old ways when it is convenient. Sort of like when white slave owners would take the Bible and quote from Paul: "Slaves be obedient to your masters and remain slaves."

I know Paul had to grow in grace and in the knowledge of the Lord like everyone else. He wasn't perfect, and neither are we. This is the same man who'd been persecuting the church, traveling from town to town having Christians put to death in the name of God—that is, until Jesus knocked him down on the Damascus Road. I know that Paul did not hold on to his Jewish customs and traditions too long, because later in life he saw a need for sisters to speak, not only in the church but also wherever they were needed to do God's work.

Later in Galatians 3:27–28 Paul said, "For as many of you as have been baptized into Christ have put on Christ. There is neither Jew, nor Greek, there is neither bond nor free, there is neither male nor female: for ye are all one in Christ Jesus." It was Paul who commended Phoebe to the church as a deacon. It was Paul who encouraged Priscilla and Aquilla to instruct Apollos in the gospel of Jesus Christ. It was Paul who began acknowledging the ministries and work of sisters in the early church. He encouraged Junia, Tryphaena, Persis, Tryphosa, the mother of Rufus, Julia, the sister of Nereus, Lydia, and all the women who did things to help build up the church, not tear it down.

Do not allow ancient traditional or cultural interpretations of the biblical role of women to hinder you from doing any work in our world that would serve to strengthen our families, save our children, and uplift our race. Sisters, this is not a time for silence! We live in a day and age when every voice must be heard and everyone deserves to sit at the table. Your Inner Eve was not afraid to speak up and talk to a snake, and neither should you silence her now. Let God's feminine voice be heard speaking out against the injustices and inequities in our world through you and in your voice.

No Silence on Violence

On October 30, 2003, sixteen-year-old Devin M. Fowlkes, a star football player at Anacostia High School in Washington, DC, was killed by a stray bullet when gunfire erupted outside the school at 3 P.M. Four months later Marita Michael, Devin's mother, spoke up before Congress against lifting the gun ban in the District. Congresswoman Eleanor Holmes Norton (D-DC) accompanied Ms. Michael and other citizens to call on Senate Majority Leader Bill Frist to withhold an amendment to repeal DC's handgun ban. At the press conference, Marita Michael asked in her dead son's name and in the name of her fifteen-year-old daughter, Artimitia Fowlkes, soon to enter Anacostia High School, that the laws banning guns in Washington, DC, be allowed to stand.

When we are empowered by our Inner Eve, the quietest, most introverted sister in our midst can find her voice to speak out against dangers and injustices in our communities and initiate change for many.

No Silence on Domestic Violence

Aminata is a forty-five-year-old African American woman who is a survivor of rape and domestic violence. She grew up in a small town in Oklahoma in which all the black families knew one another.

We dated six years through high school and college. Our parents knew each other. He would come over and court me, which consisted of looking at television. I'd never seen a violent side of him. He never gave any indication, sign, or warning of a violent side. When we went to college, we had problems getting along, but he was never violent. After college, we got engaged. The plan was that we would live together for the summer of '79 and get married the following year. After college he moved to Kansas to work, and the summer of '79 I went there to live with him. The first week of June, I moved in with him. Within a week we argued and then we were fighting. We were arguing, and something hit me across the face and it hurt. What was that? Then I realized I'd been hit. This was new; he'd never raised his voice at me before. We had three fights in about a five- or six-week period that summer.

In the course of our relationship I was raped. I did not call it a rape until 1999. It did not register in my mind that anytime someone forces sex upon you—it's a rape. It was the second fight we had. We'd had an argument a few days before . . . more or less, we were trying to make up from the argument. He wanted to have sex, and I did, too, but I did not want to do what he wanted, and I told him to stop, but he didn't . . . he would not stop.

After the third fight, I left. He's a big guy—six-foot-three, muscular, like a football player—and I'm small. He picked me up and threw me on the floor, and I landed on my left arm and my arm was numb for a couple of hours. I walked to the hospital about ten blocks. I went in the emergency room. This was 1979, before we had twenty-four-hour hotlines and shelters to call for help. The police came and asked if I wanted to press charges, and I said no, because he was standing in the door looking at me, and I was scared. I knew then that it was time to go. He picked me up and threw me to the floor like a doll—it could have been my head instead of my arm—it was time to leave.

I managed to leave because I had a safety plan. I got Jane, a white college friend, to help me. I called her and told her what was up. I told her "I need *you* to help me." Meaning, *I need you, a white woman, to help me, because if he comes back from work while we're getting my stuff out of the house, he's not going to hit a white woman in Kansas in 1979 and live to tell it.* She knew what I meant. She came and we were all packed up. As we were getting the last box out of the house, he came home and stood on the porch and asked, "Where are you going?" I said, "I'm leaving." He stood in the doorway with his arm across the door so neither one of us could get out. Jane turned to him and said, "Get out of the way!" He got off the porch and left us alone. That was in 1979 and I haven't seen him since.

My self-esteem was at its lowest point. For six months I

was a basket case. I got back to school in August of 1979. I was so stressed, I did not have a period for four months. I thought if I were prettier, I could get a new boyfriend and that would be okay. I thought I'd change my hair and clothes and I'd be set.

Through prayer, and the support of loving Christian friends, Aminata has since discovered her Inner Eve. She now knows that her beauty and worth are not based upon her hairstyle or what she wears. She is God's woman, made in the image and likeness of the Divine. The Psalmist said we are "fearfully and wonderfully made" (Psalms 139:14). After discovering and nurturing her Inner Eve, Aminata devoted her gifts and graces to help other women who were victims without hope or voice, and has become a champion of domestic violence victims.

No Silence on Sexual Abuse

"My mother was in an abusive relationship," says Marla, a forty-two-year-old African American woman.

She had five kids, and I was the eldest and only girl. One day, because of the abuse, she decided to leave him and take us to the church. It was a cold winter's day; the snow was above my head. My mother had on a thin winter coat. When she asked her pastor for help, his advice was for her to go back home to her husband. He told her it was her responsibility to be a wife and submit herself to her husband. I refuse to believe that the God I know and cherish would want any child to be subjected to physical or mental abuse. It was a long time before we went back to the church. She couldn't talk to anybody at the church, because they would say the same thing. Her closest friends and neighbors would say "You have to go back there."

From the time I was nine until I was fourteen, I was being touched by my stepfather. I started developing early, and he took an interest in me. When my mother would leave to go to the grocery store, he would tell her to leave me at home with him. What he started doing was laying me on top of him, touching me and telling me I was Daddy's little girl, and that I was special . . .

Because of this experience, I went through so much of my life thinking that in order for me to be valued, I had to have sex with men, and that sex was love. It was not until I was thirty years old that I realized that I did not have to do that and that I did not have to do anything with anybody that I did not want to.

Today Marla is a sex educator who works with youths on issues related to teen pregnancy prevention. She is committed to educating the faith community about the importance of comprehensive sexuality education.

The situation with Marla's mother could have been a wonderful opportunity for the church to be a safe haven for a battered wife and her abused children. If only the people of the church knew that intervention in domestic violence *is* ministry. If only the women of the church had the empowerment of voice, knowledge, and action to speak out about such tragedy in the life of one of their own. Rather than a passive pastor sending them back home, they could have believed Marla, knowing that her description of the violence was only the tip of the iceberg.

They could have reassured her that this was not her fault, she didn't deserve such treatment, and it was not God's will for her. They could have referred her to a battered women's service or shelter, and given her the number to a hotline. Unfortunately, none of this was done because the church is so often silent on such matters.

EVE, NO LONGER SILENT

Just as we've read in Ecclesiastes 3:7 that "There is a time to keep silence, and a time to speak," women, inspired by their Inner Eve, have found their voice and realized the power of speaking up and living out their lives to uplift girls and women everywhere. Women can no longer be held back by sexist interpretations of the scriptures saying *Women should be silent.* When we look at the great needs around us, we cannot sit silent or idle. We must use all of our resources, influence, power, and love to make life a wonderful and transforming experience for all people—especially our girls.

Sojourner Truth, an African American and former slave, delivered her "Ain't I a Woman?" speech at the 1851 Women's Convention in Akron, Ohio. She proclaimed, "If the first woman God ever made was strong enough to turn the world upside down all alone, these women together ought to be able to turn it back, and get it right side up again! And now they is asking to do it, the men better let them." Well, Sister Sojourner spoke a powerful word in 1851; how can we continue to be silent in 2005 when so many challenges stare us in the face? If God's first woman, Eve, was able to turn the world upside down, what limits do we have on turning the world right-side up? None.

INWARD REFLECTION

The mask I wear is one I've become committed to and her name is Silence.

—PORTIA SMITH

Now that we know the importance of speaking out, let's reflect and consider what message of power and change our Inner Eve wants to proclaim.

What have you been silent about in your life? Is there something you want to shout from the mountaintops?

Who has silenced your voice? Are you the culprit?

Usually we are silenced by fear. What are you afraid of? If the fear was removed, what would you boldly say and to whom?

I John 4:18 says, "Perfect love casts out fear." God is love; let God help you find your voice!

Susanism

"This is not a time for silence!"

Chapter Five

WHEN POOLS HAVE LOST THEIR PURPOSE

EVE'S EPIPHANY

John 5:1–9

In the ancient world, explorers found people practicing well-organized mind-over-matter systems to heal the sick, to bring rain, to bring fertility to their crops, and to bring success in hunting and in battle. This belief of the power of mind over matter is instinctive and universal. Even now when I am with friends and I want them to do something that they don't want to do, I usually jokingly reply, "Yes you can, it's mind over matter. I don't mind, and you don't matter."

Seriously, there is a connection between the health of the mind and the wholeness of the body. A person suffering from a psychosomatic illness has experienced some trauma to the *psyche* (Greek for "mind") that was so devastating that some *dis-ease* is manifested in the *soma* (Greek for "body"). In the Gospel of John, chapter 5, we find such a person.

Our story begins with Jesus traveling to Jerusalem for one of the Jewish feast days. He stops at a pool called Bethesda. The scene is similar to a courtyard area, with five porches surrounding a central pool of water or natural spring. On these porches lie hundreds of people who are suffering from various ailments. Some are crippled, without limbs. Some are blind. Still others are suffering from extreme arthritis, cancer, osteoporosis, paralysis, nervous disorders, degenerative disc disease, heart disease, and more. These are people whose lives have been derailed by some accident, paralyzed by some predicament, or withered while waiting for a miracle.

That is, until today, when Jesus stops by Bethesda. Now, there is a local myth or belief that at certain times of the year, an angel comes down and stirs the waters at Bethesda. Whoever is the first one in the waters after the angel comes will be healed of whatever disease he or she has. It is here, by this pool, where the paralyzed people pray for power to walk. And it is here that Jesus steps into their lives.

The Gospel writer does not tell us the name of this sick man. We don't know his race or nationality. We don't know anything about his vocation, or his values. We don't know if he has a wife or children. All we know is that he has an illness, and has been lying by this pool for thirty-eight long years waiting for a miracle, and today Jesus stands before him. The Bible says, "When Jesus saw him lie, and knew that he had been now a long time in that case, he saith unto him, 'Wilt thou be made whole?' The impotent man answered him, 'Sir; I have no man, when the water is troubled, to put me into the pool: but while I am coming, another steppeth down before me.' Jesus saith unto him, 'Rise, take up thy bed, and walk.' And immediately the man was made whole, and took up his bed, and walked: and on the same day was the Sabbath" (John 5:6–9).

Isn't that just like Jesus? Before he even speaks to the man, he already knows how long he's been there and why. When we are in the midst of our trials, tribulations, changes of life, whirlwinds, breakdowns, and personal Bermuda Triangles—God already knows our story. Our drama is new and earth-shattering to us, but not to God. There are just some things we have to go through before *we are able* to see God standing before us with the power to deliver us. We have to first realize we're lost in order to be found. We must know that we are *dis-eased* before we can be healed. It is more exciting and fulfilling when we participate in our healing, by granting our inner consent for God's Spirit to move in our lives.

Jesus says, "Ask and it shall be given you; seek, and ye shall find; knock and it shall be opened unto you: for every one that asketh receiveth; and he that seeketh findeth; and to him that knocketh it shall be opened" (Matthew 7:7–8).

Now, you may be asking, *What does this story have to do with my Inner Eve?* Everything. Clearly there are a few things going on in this man's mind, heart, and soul that have kept him in the same place for thirty-eight years, and as the daughters of Eve, we sometimes get stuck in an unhealthy place for years because we don't listen to our Inner Eve, God's voice, saying, "Rise, take up your bed and walk!" Let's look closer at this encounter between Jesus and this man, and see what we discover about ourselves.

If this man's body has been crippled and impotent for thirty-eight years, I believe that his mind and spirit have been just as broken. We don't know his story prior to this day. We don't know whether his body failed him and he lost his will to move beyond the pool, or if he lost his will and then his body failed. All we know is that he has been in this unhealthy, broken condition for a long time.

Jesus comes to him and asks, "Do you want to be made whole?" But apparently what the man hears is, "Why are you lying here?" He probably once crawled to the pool every day, or had someone bring him. Eventually either he got tired of crawling, or the folks who used to carry him got tired of bringing him. So some good Talmud-reading, Torah-keeping Jewish friends probably suggested that he get a futon, buy waterfront property, and live poolside. I'm sure they reasoned with him, saying, "What if the angel comes while you're at home?"

So he conforms to his predicament and centers his entire life on getting to the pool first, after the angel's visitation. The man's focus has been totally diverted from his brokenness to an obsession with getting from point A to point B. What he does not realize in his spiritual myopia is that his problem is not transportation, but transformation. Over these thirty-eight years he's developed a pool mentality. He's lost sight of his original reason for coming to the pool—to get healed, and be made whole. I would think that after the first two years or so, if he had not been successful in getting healed, it was time to design a new plan, formalize a new strategy, retreat, regroup, renew, and revive. But nooooooooooooooo, not Mr. *"I-don't-have-*

anybody-to-put-me-in-the-water." Talk about disabling conditions of the spirit—pool mentality will cripple your life every time.

Pool mentality makes you conform to your present situation no matter how awful it may be. You never think of alternatives to your problem. The only solution you can think of is the pool—whatever and wherever your pool is. Pool mentality makes you think that having another child will make your husband spend more time at home. Pool mentality tells you that if you keep on doing the same thing over and over and over again, one day things will change. Isn't that someone's definition of insanity? Pool mentality makes you believe that when the same difficulty arises on your new job that existed on your former job, the problem lies with the people in your office, not you. Therefore, you change jobs again—pool mentality! Pool mentality will have you lying to yourself about your problems and masquerading around town as if all is well, when your soul is about to give way. You've turned into a Pool Fool!

Jesus asks this man a yes-or-no question: "Wilt thou be made whole?" This brother is so used to people talking to him about his condition and not trying to help him out of it that he's become trained to rehearse his malady. So he tells Jesus that every time the angel comes, someone else gets in the water before he can crawl over there. For thirty-eight years. Aren't we like that sometimes? God comes to us ready to offer an opened window, a new pathway to life, a door of deliverance and transformation, but we are not attuned to hear the words of power, strength, and hope.

"Wilt thou be made whole?" This may seem like an easy

question to answer. Of course sick people want to be healed and whole again—right? Well, not necessarily. Some find comfort in staying in the same place and situation. No matter how bad it is, it's what we know. It's familiar. This man knows what to expect every day. Someone will bring him to the pool, help him sharpen his pencils to sell, bring him his meals, and let him sit there and chat with the other diseased people about their problems while eyeing the water and waiting for the angel.

Often what we think we need to be healed of, or delivered from, is not what God sees as our need. What if this man makes it to the pool after the angel stirs the water and, sitting there wet from the water, struggles to stand—and realizes that his legs are still crippled? What then? Maybe it's not his legs that are causing his problem, but his view that without the ability to walk he is less than a man and therefore life is over for him. God can use some of us better in a wheelchair with a powerful sense of self-worth than walking around with no sense of our divinity within.

So Jesus looks at the man in compassion and says, "Rise, take up your bed and walk!" The Bible tells us that he immediately stands, picks up his mat, and walks. Like this man, many of us are *dis-eased* and haven't had the luxury of time or space to stop and do something about it. *Webster's Dictionary* defines *disease* as "a condition of the body that impairs normal functioning; harmful to the well-being of a person." To be *dis-eased* is to not be at ease. Something is present in the body, mind, soul, or spirit of your life that is impairing wholeness. Not all illnesses are solely physical. As I said earlier, there can be sickness in the mind and spirit that may manifest as illness in the body. The key is to heal your whole person and assist in recovering your life.

When Jesus heals this man, he does not say, *According to your faith*. It's not a question of this man's faith in God; it's a question of his faith in himself. He has to decide he wants to be made whole, and let Jesus know he wants to be healed. He has to think about whether he wants to be able to go back to his community and be a responsible member of society—working for his income, taking a wife, and raising children. He needs to make a choice whether to be taken care of for the rest of his life, holding on to the myth of a miracle, or to participate this day in his own miracle by saying "Yes, Lord!" to Jesus, standing up, and walking.

There are women who are spiritually stuck because of some disease in their lives. Are you dis-eased? Oh yes, you may have an excellent career; a figure that is the envy of everyone at the gym; the house, the car, perfect children, a loving partner, and the credit rating of Oprah, but there is still a dis-ease on the inside. Are you disillusioned? Dispassionate? Displaced? Discouraged? Disabled? Dismayed? Disappointed? Disconnected? Distracted? Disoriented, or feel just plain old *dissed*?

To suffer from any of these conditions is to live less than an abundant life. If you are dispassionate, you are without any passion or feeling for your surroundings. To be discouraged is to be without confidence or courage in what you say and do. All women must begin to put their health, wellness, and sanity first in their lives. "Wilt thou be made whole?" is a question of will. Do you want to be healed? Do you want to be whole? It is not always the posture of the body that signals health, but rather the position of your mind and soul. You must desire something new and amazing for yourself. You must want wholeness and transformation of your life. Do you want to change the direction and focus of your life? Do you want more for yourself? Do you believe there are greater things for you?

Women are God's vessels for new life and nurturance, but we cannot effectively take care of the lives of others and nurture others if we are spiritually malnourished and anorexic ourselves. We must become whole. We must take care of ourselves and tend to our own wounds before we turn and strengthen others. If as a mother you are whole, then your children will receive the highest care and love. If as a partner you are loving yourself first, being aware of your personal needs, and finding the resources to bolster your life, then you will be a greater lover, wife, partner, and friend. As the bearers of life's sacred gifts of reproduction, intuition, and nurturance, we cannot afford to be last in line; we must be first. This is not an act of selfishness, but an act of worship. If we truly believe that our bodies are the temples of God, then we should reverence God through the care and love of ourselves.

LEARNING HOW TO BE

It has been said, "Life is not a getting and having, but a being and becoming." We are so busy *doing* life that we don't have time to live our lives. While it is important to use our skills, talents, and resources to transform our world into a better place, we cannot do any of this if we neglect to transform our own lives. It's time to stop and just *be*. You know, call in to work and take a day off. Clear your calendar. Reschedule the meeting. Let one of the other mothers pick up the kids from soccer practice today. Just switch with someone. The world will not come to an end if you are not at the meeting today. As a matter of fact, your world will begin to renew and re-create itself.

That's what *recreation* means—a time and space for the activity of re-creating yourself. When was the last time you woke up in the morning and just lay there in bed, not thinking of the million things you've got to do today, but rather about what you're going to do for yourself today? Okay, some of you may have to get up and get the kids off to school, but after that, come back home and *be* in your home a bit. Rediscover your favorite music that you hardly ever get a chance to play. Put it on, relax, and listen. Sit in your favorite spot. Drink a cup of tea, coffee, or whatever (remember, it's still morning and we've got a lot of *be-ing* to do).

I'm writing to encourage you, my sisters, to take time off to rest and be, and yet I have not done this for myself. I was wondering why I cannot seem to bring my thoughts together to finish this last section of this book, and I realized it's because I'm tired. I have not taken time out for myself in the last few weeks. I have not had time for Susan to just *be*. I'm giving advice that I'm not following. I'm so busy ministering to others, and my own needs are left unmet. I'm flying around the country preaching at churches, speaking at women's retreats, motivating youth, and I need some motivation.

As a forty-seven-year-old woman with a maturing mother, I'm realizing my new role as caregiver. No one really prepares you for the day when you see your usually vibrant and active parent move slower than normal. Nothing prepares you for seeing your mother simply unable to do normal everyday things like vacuuming and grocery shopping the way she used to. So now each day is filled with what I must do not only as a minister, a pastoral counselor, a teacher, a motivator, and an adviser to the mayor of Washington, DC, but also as a daughter whose mother needs the same care and attention that I received as a child. Understand that Momma is not feeble by any stretch of the imagination. She still lives alone, drives some places when traffic is not heavy, and hangs out with her friends and nieces. But it's there in small ways, and I can choose to ignore it or embrace the reality of the role reversal of our caregiving relationship, and plan my time of *be-ing* around it.

In my new awareness of the importance of *being* whole, nurtured, centered, and sane, I choose to embrace this new reality in my life, and order my days so that what needs to be done is done in the most loving, wise fashion for my life. It's so hard for me to put my needs first. I'm so used to placing everything else before me. I've been such a people pleaser that I feel almost guilty thinking this way. But when I am refreshed, and renewed, I am able to accomplish so much more for others.

I'm here in Hampton, Virginia, at the invitation of Dr. William Booth, to preach for First Baptist Church's Women's Day tomorrow morning. I brought my laptop so I could work on this book. I've been rushing so much, and wanted to take every opportunity alone to write. Some of the members met me at the airport, took me to dinner, and brought me to the hotel. When I entered my room there was a wonderful gift basket tied with a beautiful mauve-and-white bow, filled with butter cookies, herbal tea, a mauve-and-white china teacup and saucer, a candle, mints, and notepaper. What a wonderful surprise.

I walked into the bathroom and there was the largest bathtub I'd ever seen. It was big enough for three adult people. Normally I would thank the folks for the gift, then take it home and place it on a shelf to use *one day*. But as I sat down to write, I realized I needed to use my gift *today*. I needed to stop working for a while and just *be*. So I opened the basket, heated hot water in the room, and made a cup of tea. I drew my bath with scented bath salts, and placed the lighted candle beside it. I soaked in lavender bubbles, sipping hot tea and eating butter cookies. I was comforted by the candle's soft light and soothed by Luther's voice from the radio. For the first time in three weeks I consciously began to *be*.

8 STEPS FOR HOW TO BE

1. BE STILL. You cannot find direction or be open to Spirit's guidance if you're always doing something. You must have a time every day when you pause, be still, and meditate. Listen for Eve's voice and feel God's presence and power within.

2. BE REAL. Make a conscious commitment to take an honest look at yourself and be real about what you see. Identify the various disguises you've worn over the years, trying to conform to what others expect of you rather than being who you really are. Look at the various façades you've worn over the years, or still wear. As you acknowledge and understand each one, you will also be able to see past them to your original self, your truest self—your Inner Eve.

3. BELIEVE. Have faith in your ability to start anew from right here, where you are today. Believe that God is able to transform your present life—your very being—into something more wonderful than you've ever imagined. But know that you must grant Spirit your inner consent. It is according to *your* faith. God is able, if you are willing.

4. BE FORGETFUL. Let go of the past. Review it, journal about it, grieve it, seek counseling with someone around the issues that may arise—then leave it. All those bad experiences from childhood, failed relationships, poor choices, old jobs—leave them in the past. Bless them and let them go. If we truly believe that "All things work together for the good, to them who love God and are the called according to God's purpose" (Romans 8:28), then we must live like it. It was bad while it was happening, but God was working it for a future good. Learn from it and leave it. "Forgetting those things which are behind, and reaching forth unto those things which are before, I press toward the mark for the prize of the high calling of God in Christ Jesus" (Philippians 3:13–14).

5. BE PRESENT. Relish what new experiences Spirit has brought you today. Savor each moment in this present hour. Choose one thing you want to accomplish today, and plan your activities around it. Bring an entire project to completion, or at least move it to the next level. Live this day as if it were your last, and go to bed tonight with no regrets.

6. BE PREPARED. Always have a plan B. It's good to have a strategy for what you want to accomplish in plan A, but it is better to have a plan B for when the unexpected shows up. Don't let new things rock your world. Stand firm on your unshakable faith that "I can do all things through Christ who strengthens me" (Philippians 4:13). Remember, what doesn't kill you will only make you stronger!

7. BEHAVE like the goddess you are. The Bible says "Greater is He that's in you, than He that's in the world" (I John 4:4). Well, speaking in inclusive language and honoring the feminine expression of God's Spirit, I want to paraphrase to say, "Greater is She that is in you." God's Spirit has often felt like a nurturing mother, and I want to honor God by living like a goddess. Claim your divinity and walk in it every day, because you are fearfully and wonderfully made.

8. BEGIN. In biblical numerology, eight is the number for new beginnings. After seven years, seven months, seven days, or seven minutes of *whatever,* you can begin all over again. A clean slate is always available for you to etch life's next moment upon. A clean canvas is yielded and still for your next brushstroke. No matter what you have gone through and experienced, a new day full of possibilities awaits. Beginnings are full of promise, potential, and prosperity for your whole being. The only things you should carry over to your new beginning are the lessons learned from the past and the gifts and graces acquired along the way. Ready, set, go! "And when these things *begin* to come to pass, then look up, and lift up your heads; for your redemption draweth nigh" (Luke 21:28, emphasis added).

The Apostle Paul said, "I beseech you therefore, by the mercies of God, that ye present your bodies a living sacrifice, holy, acceptable unto God, which is your reasonable service. And be not conformed to this world: but be ye transformed by the renewing of your mind, that ye may prove what is that good, and acceptable, and perfect, will of God" (Romans 12:1–2). We have the power every day to choose how we will live our lives, how we will be transformed into God's divine idea of who we were really meant to be. We must begin behaving like women who have the spark of the divine residing within us. Being true to our Inner Eve, we must constantly be attuned to the voice of God saying to us, "Rise and walk!"

The Reverend Dr. Howard Thurman tells a story about a group of little brown caterpillars that used to play together every day, crawling around tree limbs, munching on leaves, tumbling onto the ground, and crawling into holes. They enjoyed their existence. Then one day one of them disappears; several days later he returns with wings of beautiful color, and he is flying. They greet him and admire his lovely wings and color. They invite him to play with them, but he's unable to fold his wings and crawl into holes like before. When he walks with them, the wind blows and pushes his wings against their little bodies. When it rains, his wings drag in the mud, and they admonish him, saying "Stop pushing us. We used to think you were so beautiful, but look at your muddy wings now. What good are wings anyway?" So the winged caterpillar flies away and is found days later on the petals of a rose, dead. His friends think he's died from drinking too much nectar. But he really died from a broken heart, because he had butterfly wings and a caterpillar mentality.

When God has transformed us into new creatures, we must

be true to ourselves and live as God has ordained us to live. We cannot afford to deny our divinity and live like hopeless, helpless, and hindered women. We must always be real, be forgetful, be prepared, be still, be present, and believe that we serve a God who is "able to do exceeding, abundantly above anything we can ask, think or imagine, according to the power that works in us" (Ephesians 3:20). Rise and walk!

INWARD REFLECTION

*Every human soul in the world has truth within it but
according to the conditions of the world that truth has
become hidden. When we let our intellects become free from
the past and practice sitting in silence, we can feel our
intellect become peaceful and experience love, power and
truth return inside our being.*

— DADI JANKI

**Knowing that there is a time and place for all things,
let's reflect and consider our Inner Eve's
need for a time of silence.**

Psalms 46:10 says, "Be still, and know that I am God!" God is inviting us to a time of communion through meditation. Richard J. Foster in his book *Celebration of Discipline* says, "If we hope to move beyond the superficialities of our culture, including our religious culture, we must be willing to go down into

the recreating silences, into the inner world of contempla-
tion." As Christians, our purpose in meditation is not to experience a *detachment* from the world, but rather to seek a greater
attachment to God. Christian meditation is the ability to hear
God's voice, feel God's presence, and be still with God.

To begin, sit comfortably, with your back erect. You can sit
on a chair or on floor cushions. Some prefer lying down. Close
your eyes and take a few deep breaths, feeling the breath as it
enters your nostrils and fills your body; then slowly release it.
Allow your breath to become natural, without forcing it or
controlling it. Focus on one breath at a time.

Do not become concerned if your mind wanders; that's natural. It's as if your mind is walking around the room, deciding
where to sit down and calm itself. Acknowledge whatever
sound has caught your mind's attention, and then bring it back
to its place of centering through your breathing. In like manner, meditation helps us acknowledge our mistakes in life, be
gentle and forgiving with ourselves, and move on.

Sometimes you will experience a feeling of deep con-
tentment and peace. Other times your mind may be full of
thoughts, or you may become bored and sleepy. You may experience old memories, or thoughts of people long ago forgotten.
All of this is normal. Do not be discouraged. Our subcon-
scious mind has a vast array of things to introduce to our
conscious mind. Always concentrate on bringing your mind to
a place of centered awareness of lovingkindness in your life,
and the presence of God's peace, love, and power.

You decide when is best for you to meditate. Begin with a twenty-minute session and progress to longer periods of time. It may be easier for you to meditate early in the morning before the noises of the day clamor upon you. As you mature in the practice of centering down and listening to the silence, you should be able to meditate anywhere, anytime.

Susanism

"Be a verb!"

Chapter Six

THE GODDESS WITHIN

EVE RENEWED

*Rituals create moments where living
becomes art. Poets, writers, painters and
musicians aspire to heightened moments of
awareness, times when they feel they
have something unique and inspiring to
give the world. . . . We all have this instinct
to create beauty, distinction, and
meaning in our lives. . . .*

—ALEXANDRA STODDARD,
LIVING A BEAUTIFUL LIFE

As women of spirit, love, and life, we cannot afford to be in the back of the line. For too long we have taken care of everything and everyone before caring for ourselves. Our utmost priorities have always been our children, our significant other, our parents, our job, our club, our church, and our pastor. This must stop right now.

When Jesus said, "The last shall be first, and the first last" (Matthew 20:16), he did not mean for you to go to the end of the line. The greatest commandment, says Jesus, is "Thou shalt love the Lord thy God with all thy heart, and with all thy soul, and with all thy mind. This is the first and great commandment. And the second is like unto it, Thou shalt love thy neighbor as thyself" (Matthew 22:37–39). Many of us do not sufficiently love ourselves and therefore can never *really* love others as we ought. We're just on empty. It becomes increasingly difficult to exist on the fumes of what energy we used to have. It's time to stop feeling guilty about putting your needs for nourishment and renewal first. If we understood that we do possess the divinity of God within us—we'd be unstoppable.

The Feminine Expression of God in Christianity

Feminine attributes of God are not totally foreign to Christianity. In the Bible several scriptures describe God's characteristics with feminine imagery. In Luke 13:34, God is viewed as a mother hen:

> O Jerusalem, Jerusalem, which kills the prophets, and stones them that are sent unto thee; how often would I have gathered thy children together, as a hen doth gather her brood under her wings, and ye would not!

In Isaiah 49:14–15, God is compared to a nursing mother with her infant:

> But Zion said, The Lord hath forsaken me, and my Lord hath forgotten me. Can a woman forget her sucking child, that she should not have compassion on the son of her womb? Yea, they may forget, yet will I not forget thee.

In Deuteronomy 32:11–12, God is seen as a mother eagle, bearing up her babies:

As an eagle stirs up her nest, flutters over her young, spreads abroad her wings, takes them, and bears them on her wings: So the Lord alone did lead him.

GOD AS MOTHER AND YOUR INNER EVE

In Christianity, God is usually referred to as *He* and *Father*. The worship of God in the form of Mother, however, is a feature of Hinduism and other Eastern religions. Through the ages, the doctrine of the Motherhood of God has been established firmly in Hinduism. By worshiping God as the Divine Mother, a Hindu can more easily attribute motherly traits to the Lord, such as tenderness and forgiveness. The natural love between a mother and her child is the best expression of the Lord's unconditional love for us as children of God. In the most representative Hindu view, the universe is the manifestation of the creative power (Shakti) of God. This is what I call your Inner Eve—God's feminine creative power and spiritual presence inside us.

To a Hindu, the motherly aspect of God in nature is full of beauty, gentleness, kindness, and tenderness. When we look upon all the glorious and beautiful things of nature and feel tenderness within us, we are experiencing the motherly instinct of God. When a Hindu worships God as Divine Mother, he or she appeals to her tenderness and unconditional love. Such love unites the devotee with God, like a child with its mother. Just as a child feels safe and secure in the lap of its mother, a devotee feels safe and secure in the presence of the Divine Mother.

The worship of God as Mother has had a significant impact on Hinduism. The position of women in the Hindu religion is dignified because each woman is considered a manifestation of the Divine Mother. Hindus view man and woman as the two wings of the same bird. Thus, a man is considered incomplete without a woman, since—according to Swami Vivekananda— "it is not possible for a bird to fly on only one wing." Through the worship of God in the form of Mother, Hinduism offers a unique reverence of womanhood.

THE GODDESS IN US

As Christians we worship God as a Spirit, and they who worship God must do so in spirit and truth. The Bible teaches that we are made in the image and likeness of God; therefore, I must believe that there is a male and female expression of God. When I look into the mirror I see God's expression in Susan, and you, too, should see God's expression in yourself. The most critical aspect of my spiritual walk with God knows that God's presence is within me to nurture, inspire, guide, and empower me. God's presence in me is there to calm me, fulfill me, encourage me, strengthen me, uphold me, and teach me. I have access to all of God's characteristics through my choice to seek, find, and be in relationship with my Inner Eve.

Rituals of Renewal for Your Inner Eve

Any good relationship is established and strengthened through time and intimacy. In order to get to know someone, you must spend time with him or her. You gain greater knowledge of yourself and your Inner Eve through a special time I like to call a *ritual of renewal*.

Sisters, what do you do for joy? When was the last time you had a ritual of renewal for yourself? When most of us hear the word *ritual*, images of candles, symbols, and altars come to mind. That's very true for many, but according to *Merriam-Webster's Dictionary*, a *ritual* is "a customary repeated series of acts." It does not have to be overtly religious to be spiritually beneficial.

When was the last time you nurtured your Inner Eve? I found out at the age of forty-five that my Inner Eve is nurtured when I do something joyous for me. That sounds simple enough, but it was earth-shattering information for me. I'm always doing something for others. I'm sure I have good company. There are women who will put everything and everyone else's needs before their own needs and happiness.

I have always loved to dance, but for years I danced only in my home because I was self-conscious about my body. A few years ago I decided I was going to take dance lessons and go out dancing, no matter what anyone else thought about me. I signed up for classes in Hand Dancing—a form of swing dance—in Washington, DC. It involves a six-count dance with a lot of footwork while you hold your partner's hand. It's a lead-follow dance with twists, turns, dips, and lifts, and I love it. I've lost more than sixty-five pounds, and the dancing helps me keep it off. Interesting enough, as a single woman without a boyfriend, it affords me the benefit of being in a man's arms a couple of days a week—even if it is just until the song ends! My Inner Eve wanted to dance, and I said yes.

We all have some ritual or act of worship that we perform inwardly and outwardly to wash ourselves from the drudgery of our days and the mediocrity of our moments. Sometimes we do it early in the morning, in the afternoon at work, or in the evening. Think about developing a ritual of renewal for your Inner Eve. How can you bring new joy into your life? You will be transformed spiritually and empowered from within by simply doing one act of joy for yourself each week.

In thinking about your ritual for renewal, think of where you want it to take place. Do you want to be on your porch, in the bathtub, or in the park? What things do you wish to have with you? Music? Candles? Symbols? Are you alone or in a group? How often do you perform your ritual? I asked a few sisterfriends to share their rituals with you. You'll be surprised what some of us do to renew ourselves and what brings joy into our todays. If you don't have a ritual of your own, I invite you to try one of these until yours shows up.

CONNIE, 50, HAGERSTOWN, MARYLAND

I'm renewed through what I like to call "Great Escapes Through Self-Indulgence." I like to pick a favorite actor or actress or theme, such as mysteries or musicals; get a favorite snack (popcorn, brownies, or ice cream); and have a marathon of my favorite movies and books. I went to a video store and rented all the Dolly Parton movies and had myself a Dolly Marathon. The same with books—I love reading romance novels, even more so if they have a touch of the supernatural or mystery. On a "welcoming" day such as the beginning of spring or in the dead of winter with lots of snow on the ground but the sun is out, I like to take time out to read a favorite author or theme from cover to cover with no other sounds in the house.

TaRESSA, 49, SOUTHERN NEW JERSEY

I'm not as organized or consistent as I fantasize about being with my renewal rituals, but what I end up doing includes:

∽ Reading magazines, usually with a cup of hot tea, either when I can steal a quiet moment at home or while one of my children is playing basketball or doing gymnastics.

ᵉ Watching the TV series *Soul Food,* to which I am totally addicted. Each episode is as good as a full-length movie and leaves me feeling serene and joyous.

ᵉ Long, hot bubble baths or showers . . . topped off with a shampoo. Water soothes and renews me every time.

ᵉ A pedicure at the corner salon makes me feel as if I've got it all together.

ᵉ Dancing; most recently, belly-dancing classes. This ancient African form of personal and spiritual expression and celebration of the Divine Feminine Self untangles my mental knots and realigns my chakras until I'm glowing.

CLAUDETTE, 48, REISTERSTOWN, MARYLAND

My mom passed away from breast cancer when I was eleven years old. I have never known my father and I am the youngest of five children. My oldest sister, Gwen, is twenty years older than me and lives in Maryland with her family. After my mom died, I moved from California to Maryland to live with my sister and her family. I remember one day in sixth grade I was sitting alone in the house and saw a little angel figurine that my sister had on a table in the living room. I stared at that angel, and my soul began to drift away. In an instant, I saw a vision of my mother. I felt as though I was hallucinating, so I closed my eyes really tight and opened them up again . . . the vision was still there, and this time I could hear her voice saying "God is Light."

From that day forward, I began to look at all angels in a different light. I wanted to collect them and surround myself with them because I felt like, with them, I would have God and my mother right next to me. It's not as if I see my mother's face each time I look at one, but the memory of that first vision comes to mind when I think about it. In time, God has revealed to me what that original experience in the living room meant to me.

Each day now I pray in front of a small shelf that I have with about eight angels. One of the angels is a lady with a child next to her, which reminds me of my mother and me. Somehow with everything I have been through, my spirit is renewed every day. There are two scriptures in the Bible that I favor because I think they speak to me each time I pray. "This then is the message which we have heard of him, and declare unto you, that God is light, and in him is no darkness at all" (I John 1:5). The second one is my mother's favorite: "If you have faith as small as a mustard seed, nothing will be impossible for you" (Matthew 17:20). With the angels and these passages, I feel the presence of my mother even though she is no longer with me. Even though she has not been with me, she has given me to a greater source that has been all I have ever really needed.

Tamara, 45, Atlanta

I begin each day in my bedroom, in a prayer of thanksgiving to God. Then I read the appropriate daily message from Iyanla Vanzant's *Acts of Faith*. During the summer of 2002, after consulting a Yoruba priestess in New Orleans, I created an altar in the guest room of our home. It is a small table covered with a white, embroidered blanket. On the altar I have placed a collection of seashells; rare stones and pebbles; white candles; nine six-ounce glasses of water; a medium-sized brandy glass of water; a gold cross that covers the brandy glass; a beautiful brown twelve-inch-tall glazed ceramic angel made in 2002 by my daughter Moriah (who was eight years old at the time); and tributes to three of my favorite Spiritual Guides who have passed on: my paternal grandmother, an aunt, and a surrogate mother/mentor.

Three or four times weekly, I kneel before the altar and pray to God, the ancestors, angels, Orishas, and Spiritual Guardians. I light a white candle and burn incense in thanksgiving and praise for the numerous blessings of my life, for my health, my precious angel daughter Moriah, parents, elders, immediate and extended family and friends, as well as the enemies and negative energies I encounter daily. At least once per week, Moriah joins me in prayer.

When I arrive at work, I look out the window of my

thirty-ninth-floor office; I recite another prayer of thanks-giving and make a plea for strength, courage, and wisdom. This is my daily ritual. I would be unable to survive and thrive on the shores of this tempestuous sea were it not for my faith and confidence in God's grace.

MY RITUAL—SUSAN, 47, WASHINGTON, DC

One of my rituals for renewal is done early in the morning. Upon awakening, I get out of bed and go into my living room. I open the blinds to let the light of the sun brighten the room and warm my spirit. I light incense or scented candles (vanilla or coco-mango). Sometimes I turn on my water fountain and listen to the bubbling of the water. Sometimes I turn on cable television, which has soundscape music as one of its selec-tions. Or I turn on my wind chimes (they're electric, and I control how often the inner fan moves the chimes).

I recline on my gold cloth chaise longue, with my purple throw covering my legs. In front of me on the wall is a paint-ing: *The Prayer Messenger* by Paul Goodnight. It is of a woman of African descent wearing a very light peach-colored dress and head wrap. She is stooping down, holding a dove on her lap, as another dove flies toward them. It is as if the bird has returned from a mission of mercy, delivering her prayers of hope and wholeness to some battered and bruised spirit.

Relaxed, in a peaceful state somewhere between rest and renewal, I sit. My nostrils teased by mango candles and vanilla incense. My mind soothed by the sounds of harp and adagio piano. I think and pray. I discover things that do not benefit me, and I ask for strength to release them from my life. I talk to God, and sometimes it is as if I hear my voice for the first time, speaking from a place I never knew was inside me. I praise God for life's blessings, and pray for wisdom and insight to be God's light and love. Then my Inner Eve nudges me to get going—she has something to say today.

INWARD REFLECTION

God always meets us where we are and slowly moves us along into deeper things.

—RICHARD FOSTER

It is new and exciting to reflect and consider
the spark of the divine that resides within us.
How do we re-create our lives to embrace
and affirm our Inner Eve?

Learn to affirm yourself daily. An affirmation can be any positive statement you make about yourself. When speaking about ourselves, we usually make statements from a negative perspective. Saying "I hate my hips" will not help you love your body.

Saying, "I am open to new ways to enhance my beauty," however, will affirm your beauty and open your consciousness to creative change. You can create your world with the power of your consciousness, your words, and your Inner Eve.

Imagine how you want your life to be and make positive statements affirming it. Always speak in the active voice and in the present tense, such as *I have* or *I am*. Make a list of things that you don't like about yourself, then restate them in a positive way.

Your negative list could include . . .

   There's nothing special about me.

   Nobody loves me.

   I hate my apartment.

You can change these statements to . . .

   I am discovering wonderful things about myself such as my welcoming smile and the brilliance of my personality.

   God loves me and therefore, I am worthy of love.

   I am so blessed to have a warm place to live and a roof over my head.

Loving and affirming yourself is the greatest commandment. "Thou shall love the Lord thy God with all thy heart, and with all thy soul, and with all thy mind. This is the first and great commandment. And the second is like unto it, Thou shall love thy neighbor as thyself" (Matthew 22:37–39).

Susanism

"I create my world."

Chapter Seven

IN THE GARDEN

EVE INSPIRED

For Adam and Eve, the Garden of Eden was the place where they were created, where they were at ease and one with God. There was peace in the Garden. There was joy in the Garden. Everything they desired was available to them. Because of their disobedience to God, however, they were banished from this place of tranquility and had to live by the sweat of their brow, working the ground. Although we, like Adam and Eve, do not live in the Garden of Eden, our Inner Eve can help us realize that spiritual place within our souls where the Garden is available to us today.

When I talk about the Garden, I'm referring to that place where we feel at home. It is a place where we find joy, love, and happiness. When we're there, all is well with our soul; we feel nurtured and loved. Home is not 1838 Belmont Road, where I grew up. It's not Washington, DC. Home, like the Garden, is in our hearts. We don't have to travel far, for it is a short distance from within our minds into our hearts. It is not something that automatically grows there, but must be deliberately planted and cultivated, just as we do with a lovely plant: We take a small cutting and place it in water until it grows roots, then transplant it in the soil of our own home.

The image of my inner Garden and that feeling of being at home are so similar, I guess they really are the same for me. My Garden is my spiritual home, my soul's home. It is easier for me to feel "at home" when my soul is at ease.

We have the power of our minds to create our own Gardens. We can bring wonderful, nurturing, and inspiring thoughts and memories to our mental Gardens. For some of us, memories of home include Christmas gatherings around a table full of holiday favorites, or birthday parties and family vacations. For others, memories of home are of disappointments and fear. It has been said, "You are born into your family, but you choose your friends." Even more so, we can create new memories in our own spiritual Garden by choosing what thoughts we place there.

The Apostle Paul instructs us about the spiritual care of our minds in Philippians 4:8, saying, "Finally, brethren, whatsoever things are true, whatsoever things are honest, whatsoever things are just, whatsoever things are pure, whatsoever things are lovely, whatsoever things are of good report; if there be any virtue, and if there be any praise, think on these things." We can create our own joy by what we gather to our minds and spirits and what we surround ourselves with.

I used to feel that I'd only be happy living in a particular city or part of the country. I've traveled a lot as a preacher and motivational speaker. I've been blessed to see forty-five of the fifty states as well as parts of Europe, Africa, and the Caribbean. There have been times when I've thought about moving to another location, then I realized that I can be happy right where I am. It's not important what zip code I live in, but what kind of joy I nurture where I am. I can create my own joy.

My physical surroundings are critical for maintaining the balance and harmony in my spiritual Garden. When I moved to Atlanta, Georgia, to assume the pastorate of the First Congregational Church, I was alone. I left my family back in DC, and I only knew two or three people there. Of course everyone knew me, because I was the new "lady pastor" at the historical First Church in downtown Atlanta.

I attended all the "in" social affairs in the city and met hundreds of people. But at night I would return to my luxurious high-rise apartment in the grand Georgian Terrace in midtown Atlanta, across the street from the famed Fox Theatre, where *Gone with the Wind* premiered in 1939. I wasn't happy. I felt displaced. I did not feel *at home* in my own house. I would call my friends in New York, New Jersey, DC, and Maryland and talk on the phone for hours. I justified the expenditure because at ten cents a minute I could talk for an hour for just six dollars. That was like meeting a friend for a cup of Starbucks coffee.

It wasn't until I moved farther out in the suburbs of Atlanta, away from midtown, that my soul began to be more at ease. I bought a house that had a screened-in porch in the back.

There were only trees behind my home. I bought a swing for my porch. In the early mornings I would sit out there and listen to the invocation of the birds' songs as the sun rose. At night I would usher in the evening by sitting on my swing with candles lit, music playing, and the scent of honeysuckle in Georgia's night air. I watched as the purple-and-azure sun would set and the low-hanging harvest moon would pronounce the day's benediction. I was beginning to feel *at home*.

I began to place framed photographs of my family and friends all over the house. There were photos on the walls leading up the steps, on the counters in the living room, bedroom, and office. I began to buy myself fresh-cut flowers and put them in a large crystal vase on the kitchen counter. All of these things brought me a sense of wholeness and healing for my homesick soul. I had pictures of my mother and sister. I had pictures of my father's brothers—all six of the Reverend Newmans. I experienced a new sense of family when I framed and placed a picture of my uncle the Reverend Dr. Isaiah DeQuincy Newman on the mantel. In 1983 "I Deek," as everyone called him, was the first black man elected to the South Carolina State Senate since Reconstruction. As a child I remembered seeing his picture in *Jet* magazine with Dr. Martin Luther King Jr. I later learned he was the executive secretary of the South Carolina NAACP from 1960 to 1969. I was starting to feel at home in the South. I discovered my roots in the region.

By surrounding myself with things that reminded me of who

I was and where I came from, I began to feel connected with my family more than ever before. After I was able to create *home* in Atlanta through my spiritual Garden of memories, pictures, family, and friends, I was drawn deeper within to spend nurturing quiet time with God. My physical surroundings comforted me enough that I was now able to center and turn my attention inward to a new awareness of God in my life—my Inner Eve.

God's feminine voice beckoned me to a new experience of prayer and solitude. I found out the difference between being lonely and being alone. I was surprisingly satisfied with hours of solitude. Teresa of Avila said, "Settle yourself in solitude and you will come upon Him in yourself." I encountered not only God, but also God's presence as the Holy Spirit engaged me as a woman. It was during my spiritual gardening that I discovered my Inner Eve.

God's feminine voice called me from loneliness to a strange solitude. Even when I was around hundreds of strangers, I felt the presence of God. When no other person was near, I experienced a sweet communion in my solitude with God. I used to rush out of my house to any function just to be around people, but for this moment all my needs for companionship were supplied by God.

I now understand why Jesus spent so much time alone with his father. When you are doing so much for others, you need a sacred time and place to be refreshed and renewed in your inner spirit. Jesus began his ministry in solitude for forty days in the wilderness (Matthew 4:1–11). The night before he called his twelve disciples, Jesus spent the night alone in the desert hills (Luke 6:12). After ministering to hundreds of people late into the night, "in the morning, a great while before day, he rose and went out to a lonely place. . . ." (Mark 1:35)

As a child in Sunday school, my favorite hymn was "In the Garden."

I come to the garden alone.
While the dew is still on the roses,
And the voice I hear falling on my ear
The Son of God discloses.
And He walks with me and He talks with me.
And He tells me I am His own.
And the joy we share as we tarry there,
None other has ever known.

Every time I sing that song I can feel the intimacy of God's presence. That song, like so many hymns of the church, is woven into the fabric of my spiritual Garden. The hymns of the faithful usher me into an inner sanctum where I can hear the divine whisper. One lyricist said it well when he penned the phrase, "I can almost hear the brush of angel's wings."

In the beginning of this book I talked about my lessons from the movie *The Wizard of Oz*. There is another lesson I learned from that movie. At the end of the movie, Dorothy, in order to return home to Kansas, had to click her heels three times and say, "There's no place like home, there's no place like home, there's no place like home." I learned the importance of simple affirmations for what I wanted to create in my life, or, as the saints put it, "speak things into existence."

I began to search the Word of God for scriptures about joy. Since I was determined to create my own joy, I wanted to know what my Creator has said about it. My Joy Journey began one day when I sought the Bible, not out of joy, but from a place of despondency and pain. The promises of the Lord leapt off the pages and my healing from loneliness began as my joy grew.

BIBLICAL AFFIRMATIONS FOR YOUR JOY JOURNEY

✐ "Do not grieve, for the joy of the Lord is your strength" (Nehemiah 8:10 NIV).

✐ "Those who sow in tears will reap with songs of joy" (Psalms 126:5 NIV).

✐ "Weeping may endure for a night, but joy cometh in the morning" (Psalms 30:5 NIV).

✐ "Peace I leave you, my peace I give unto you: not as the world giveth, give I unto you. Let not your heart be troubled. . . ." (John 14:27)

✐ "He will yet fill your mouth with laughter and your lips with shouts of joy" (Job 8:21 NIV).

⁊ "As the Father has loved me, so have I loved you. Now remain in my love. If you obey my commands, you will remain in my love, just as I have obeyed my Father's commands and remain in his love. I have told you this so that my joy may be in you and that your joy may be complete" (John 15:9–11 NIV).

⁊ "You have made known to me the path of life; you will fill me with joy in your presence and with eternal pleasures at your right hand" (Psalms 16:11 NIV).

What broke the yoke of my despondency was Isaiah 61:1–3 (NIV):

The Spirit of the Sovereign Lord is on me, because the Lord has anointed me to preach good news to the poor. He has sent me to bind up the brokenhearted, to proclaim freedom for the captives and release from darkness for the prisoners, to proclaim the year of the Lord's favor and the day of vengeance of our God, to comfort all who mourn, and provide for those who grieve in Zion—to bestow on them a crown of beauty instead of ashes, the oil of gladness instead of mourning, and a garment of praise instead of a spirit of despair.

I gladly received my "crown of beauty" and rubbed the "oil of gladness" on my face. Suddenly the long night of my spiritual despair and loneliness had ended and I pranced around in my "garment of praise" to the Lord. My Inner Eve was out and beginning to have a great time through my life! You can take Eve out of the Garden, but you can't take the Garden out of Eve. My Joy Journey and sacred time of solitude and devotion with God liberated my Inner Eve and empowered my life and ministry.

The first thing on my Inner Eve's agenda was to get my body as healthy as my inner self through the help of medical science, nutrition, and exercise. Over the last few years I've gone from a size 28 dress to a size 18. I no longer sit at home despondent: I go out dancing at least twice a week for cardiovascular exercise and fun. I no longer take eight pills a day for diabetes, hypertension, high cholesterol, and joint pains. I no longer sleep with a continuous positive airway pressure machine for sleep apnea, a dreaded disease that causes you to stop breathing when you sleep. All of these were by-products of my obesity and neglect of my body. I could no longer afford to ignore my temple and focus strictly on the spiritual. I realized the critical need for a full balance in my life of loving God with my body, mind, soul, and spirit.

It was not enough for me to preach and see lives transformed by the moving of God in my life, and then go home and be wrestled to the ground by a piece of chocolate cake. My Inner Eve gave me the strength and discipline to follow what I felt was my path to health and wholeness. There is no such thing as a quick fix for any challenge in life. I believe that we can accomplish anything through the power of our determination and God's Spirit. I thank God for discovering my Inner Eve!

Now that you've prayed about your situation, it's time to unfold your praying hands and be a verb. Start where you are, use what you have, and do what you can. For this is not a time for silence. Now that you've discovered your Inner Eve, and realized that pools have lost their purpose in your life, it's time for your goddess within to come out!

INWARD REFLECTION

You can take Eve out of the Garden, but you can't take the Garden out of Eve. This is my affirmation for my Inner Eve that sprang up one day while meditating in my spiritual Garden. Reflect and consider how to create a Garden for your Inner Eve.

A WOMAN'S TRUTH

The Reverend Dr. Susan Delora Newman

I do not want a religion to hang around my neck.

I do not need to kneel anymore, sacrifice or genuflect.

Religion is dogmas, laws, and creeds—it is enough, we have too many of these.

It is pure Spirit that my soul longs for; a spiritual union is what I adore.

It is a door opening, a burden lifted, a harbor safe from the storm.

Its presence dances within us; it guides us on our way. It's the joyous realization that suffering and pain have a mission in our lives.

It is what makes us into the ones who will not bow, will not break, and will not surrender whatever it takes. We are the ones who must bare our souls lest we die, we must speak truth, and we cannot lie. We are often misunderstood, but we bear no shame, we know our passion, we claim our pain.

Love is not a subject to discuss. Love is to be felt, seen, and heard from around, above, below, and in us. It is not red hearts that we share once a year; it is not the 13th chapter of Corinthians in our ears. It is not the residue of our passion and lust. Love is the Bread of Life, from the seed to the crust.

Don't look at me, trying to understand. I am not of the stars, the sea, or the land. I am born for just a moment of eternity's span, just a spark of the miracle that God created—I am Woman!

Susanism

"Know your passion!"

RESOURCE GUIDE

Sexual Abuse and Domestic Violence

The listings below are resources for you if you are a victim of violence, or are seeking a place to volunteer and get information about working for the safety of women and children.

The Black Church and Domestic Violence Institute
1292 Ralph David Abernathy Boulevard, Suite 100
Atlanta, GA 30310
phone: 404-758-0019
fax: 404-758-9619
The Reverend Aubra Love, Director
The Reverend Aubra Love is an ordained United Church of Christ minister, and the founder and executive director of the Black Church and Domestic Violence Institute in Atlanta, Georgia. Love started this institute to educate religious leaders and other human service providers about domestic violence.

The African American Task Force Against Domestic and Sexual Violence
phone: 206-322-4856
Web site: www.aataskforce.homestead.com

National Domestic Violence Hotline
toll-free: 800-799-SAFE (7233)

National Sexual Violence Resource Center
toll-free: 877-739-3895
Web site: www.nsvrc.org
The National Sexual Violence Resource Center opened in July 2000 as a vital new center for information, resources, and research related to all aspects of sexual violence. It serves and supports state and territory coalitions, local rape crisis centers, government and tribal entities, universities, researchers, and the general public. With a large and growing library of resources, the NSVRC responds to requests for information and augments grassroots efforts to end sexual violence by distributing information and materials, including prevention tools. It coordinates efforts with other organizations and projects; provides technical assistance and customized information packets on specific topics; and maintains a Web site of current information on conferences, funding opportunities, research, and Sexual Assault Awareness Month (SAAM). The NSVRC produces a semiannual newsletter, *The Resource*, and booklets that focus on underserved populations. As a project of the Pennsylvania Coalition Against Rape (PCAR), the NSVRC provides resources and identifies emerging issues related to the difficult task of ending sexual violence.

State and Territory Coalitions

Alabama Coalition Against Rape
P.O. Box 4091
Montgomery, AL 36102
phone: 334-264-0123
toll-free: 888-725-7273
fax: 334-264-0128
Web site: www.acar.org

Alaska Network on Domestic Violence and Sexual Assault
130 Seward Street, Suite 209
Juneau, AK 99801
phone: 907-586-3650
toll-free: 800-520-2666
fax: 904-463-4493
Web site: www.andvsa.org

Arizona Sexual Assault Network
2018 North Arizona Avenue,
Suite D-140
Chandler, AZ 85225
phone: 480-814-1400
fax: 480-814-0373
Web site: www.azsan.org

Arkansas Coalition Against Sexual Assault
215 North East Avenue
Fayetteville, AR 72701
phone: 479-527-0900
toll-free: 866-632-2272
fax: 479-527-0902
Web site: www.acasa.ws

California Coalition Against Sexual Assault
1215 K Street, Suite 1100
Sacramento, CA 95814
phone: 916-446-2520
fax: 916-446-8166
Web site: www.calcasa.org

Colorado Coalition Against Sexual Assault
P.O. Box 300398
Denver, CO 80203
phone: 303-861-7033
toll-free: 877-372-2272
fax: 303-832-7067
Web site: www.ccasa.org

Connecticut Sexual Assault Crisis Services, Inc.
96 Pitkin Street
East Hartford, CT 06108

phone: 860-282-9881
toll-free: 888-999-5545
fax: 860-291-9335
Web site: www.connsacs.org

D.C. Rape Crisis Center
P.O. Box 34125
Washington, DC 20043
phone: 202-232-0789
fax: 202-387-3812
Web site: www.dcrcc.org

CONTACT Delaware, Inc.
P.O. Box 9525
Wilmington, DE 19809
phone: 302-761-9800
fax: 302-761-4280
Web site:
www.contactdelaware.org

Florida Council Against Sexual Violence
1311 Paul Russell Road,
Suite A 204
Tallahassee, FL 32301
phone: 850-297-2000
toll-free: 888-956-7273
fax: 850-297-2002
Web site: www.fcasv.org

Georgia Network to End Sexual Assault
619 Edgewood Avenue SE,
Suite 104
Atlanta, GA 30312
phone: 678-701-2700
fax: 678-701-2709
Web site: www.gnesa.org

Guam Healing Hearts Crisis Center
790 Gov. Carlos G. Camacho Road
Tamuning, GU 96911
phone: 671-647-5351
toll-free: 800-711-4826
fax: 671-649-6948
Web site:
www.pmcguam.com/news/healhart.htm

Hawaii Coalition Against Sexual Assault
P.O. Box 10596
Honolulu, HI 96816
phone: 808-733-9038
fax: 808-733-9032

Idaho Coalition Against Sexual and Domestic Violence
815 Park Boulevard, Suite 140
Boise, ID 83712
phone: 208-384-0419
toll-free: 888-293-6118
fax: 208-331-0687
Web site: www.idvsa.org

Illinois Coalition Against Sexual Assault
100 North 16th Street
Springfield, IL 62703
phone: 217-753-4117
fax: 217-753-8229
Web site: www.icasa.org

Indiana Coaltion Against Sexual Assault
55 Monument Circle, Suite 1224
Indianapolis, IN 46204
phone: 317-423-0233
toll-free: 800-691-2272
fax: 317-423-0237
Web site: www.incasa.org

Iowa Coalition Against Sexual Assault
2603 Bell Avenue, Suite 102
Des Moines, IA 50321
phone: 515-244-7424
fax: 515-244-7417
Web site: www.iowacasa.org

Kansas Coalition Against Sexual and Domestic Violence
220 SW 33rd Street, Suite 100
Topeka, KS 66611
phone: 785-232-9784
fax: 785-266-1874
Web site: www.kcsdv.org

Kentucky Association of Sexual Assault Programs, Inc.
P.O. Box 4028
Frankfort, KY 40604
phone: 502-226-2704
fax: 502-226-2725
Web site: www.kasap.org

Louisiana Foundation Against Sexual Assault
509 West Morris

Hammond, LA 70403
phone: 985-345-5995
toll-free: 888-995-7273
fax: 985-345-5592
Web site: www.lafasa.org

Maine Coalition Against Sexual Assault
83 Western Avenue, Suite 2
Augusta, ME 04330
phone: 207-626-0034
toll-free: 800-871-7741
fax: 207-626-5503
Web site: www.mecasa.org

Maryland Coalition Against Sexual Assault
1517 Governor Ritchie
Highway, Suite 207
Arnold, MD 21012
phone: 410-974-4507
toll-free: 800-983-7273
fax: 410-757-4770
Web site: www.mcasa.org

Massachusetts Coalition Against Sexual Assault and Domestic Violence
14 Beacon Street, Suite 507
Boston, MA 02108
phone: 617-248-0922
fax: 617-248-0902
Web site: www.janedoe.org

Michigan Coalition Against Domestic and Sexual Violence
3893 Okemos Road, Suite B2
Okemos, MI 48864

phone: 517-347-7000
fax: 517-347-1377
Web site: www.mcadsv.org

Minnesota Coalition Against Sexual Assault
420 North 5th Street, Suite 690
Minneapolis, MN 55401
phone: 612-313-2797
toll-free: 800-964-8847
fax: 612-313-2799
Web site: www.mncasa.org

Mississippi Coalition Against Sexual Assault
P.O. Box 4172
Jackson, MS 39296
phone: 601-948-0555
toll-free: 888-987-9011
fax: 601-948-0525
Web site: www.mcasa.net

Missouri Coalition Against Sexual Assault
P.O. Box 104866
Jefferson City, MO 65110
phone: 573-636-8776
fax: 573-636-6613
Web site:
http://mocasa.missouri.org

Montana Coalition Against Domestic and Sexual Violence
P.O. Box 633
Helena, MT 59624
phone: 406-443-7794
fax: 406-443-7818
Web site: www.mcadsv.com

Nebraska Domestic Violence Sexual Assault Coalition
825 M Street, Suite 404
Lincoln, NE 68508
phone: 402-476-6256
fax: 402-476-6806
Web site: www.ndvsac.org

Nevada Coalition Against Sexual Violence
P.O. Box 530103
Henderson, NV 89053
phone: 702-940-2033
fax: 702-940-2032
Web site: www.ncasv.org

New Hampshire Coalition Against Domestic & Sexual Violence
P.O. Box 353
Concord, NH 03302
phone: 603-224-8893
toll-free: 800-277-5570
fax: 603-228-6096
Web site: www.nhcadsv.org

New Jersey Coalition Against Sexual Assault
2333 Whitehorse-Mercerville Road, Suite B
Trenton, NJ 08619
phone: 609-631-4450
toll-free: 800-601-7200
fax: 609-631-4453
Web site: www.njcasa.org

New Mexico Coalition of Sexual Assault Programs, Inc.
3909 Juan Tabo, NE #6
Albuquerque, NM 87111
phone: 505-883-8020
toll-free: 888-883-8020
fax: 505-883-7530
Web site: www.swcp.com/nmcsaas

New York City Alliance Against Sexual Assault
411 West 114 Street, Suite 6D
New York, NY 10025
phone: 212-523-4344
fax: 212-523-4429
Web site: www.nycagainstrape.org

New York State Coalition Against Sexual Assault
63 Colvin Avenue
Albany, NY 12206
phone: 518-482-4222
fax: 518-482-4248
Web site: www.nyscasa.org

North Carolina Coalition Against Sexual Assault
4426 Louisburg Road, Suite 100
Raleigh, NC 27616
phone: 919-431-0995
toll-free: 888-737-2272
fax: 919-431-0996
Web site: www.nccasa.org

North Dakota Coalition Against Sexual Assault
418 East Rousser, #320
Bismarck, ND 58501
phone: 701-255-6240
toll-free: 888-255-6240
fax: 701-255-1904
Web site: www.ndcaws.org

Ohio Coalition on Sexual Assault
933 High Street, Suite 120-B
Worthington, OH 43085
phone: 614-781-1902
fax: 614-781-1922
Web site: www.ocosa.org

Oklahoma Coalition Against Domestic Violence and Sexual Assault
2525 NW Express Way, Suite 101
Oklahoma City, OK 73112
phone: 405-848-1815
fax: 405-848-3469
Web site: www.ocadvsa.org

Oregon Coalition Against Domestic and Sexual Violence
115 Mission Street, SE, Suite 100
Salem, OR 97302
phone: 503-365-9644
toll-free: 800-622-3782
fax: 503-566-7870
Web site: www.ocadsv.org

Pennsylvania Coalition Against Rape
125 North Enola Drive
Enola, PA 17025
phone: 717-728-9740
toll-free: 800-692-7445
fax: 717-728-9781
Web site: www.pcar.org

Coordinadora Paz Para La Mujer, Inc.
Apartado 193008
San Juan, PR 00919
phone: 787-777-0738
fax: 787-767-6843
Web site: www.pazparalamujer.org

Rhode Island Sexual Assault Coalition
300 Richmond Street, Suite 205
Providence, RI 02903
phone: 401-421-4100
fax: 401-454-5565
Web site: www.satrc.org

South Carolina Coalition Against Domestic Violence and Sexual Assault
P.O. Box 7776
Columbia, SC 29202
phone: 803-256-2900
toll-free: 800-260-9293
fax: 803-256-1030
Web site: www.sccadvasa.org

South Dakota Coalition Against Domestic Violence and Sexual Assault
P.O. Box 141
Pierre, SD 57501
phone: 605-945-0869
toll-free: 800-572-9196
fax: 605-945-0869
Web site:
www.southdakotacoalition.org

South Dakota Network Against Family Violence and Sexual Assault
P.O. Box 90453
Sioux Falls, SD 57109
phone: 605-731-0041
toll-free: 800-670-3989
fax: 605-977-4742
Web site: www.sdnafvsa.com

Tennessee Coalition Against Domestic and Sexual Violence
P.O. Box 120972
Nashville, TN 37212
phone: 615-386-9406
fax: 615-383-2967
Web site: www.tcadsv.org

Texas Association Against Sexual Assault
7701 North Lamar, Suite 104
Austin, TX 78752
phone: 512-474-7190
toll-free: 888-918-2272
fax: 512-474-6490
Web site: www.taasa.org

Utah Coalition Against Sexual Assault
284 West 400 North
Salt Lake City, UT 84103
phone: 801-746-0404
fax: 801-746-2929
Web site: www.ucasa.org

Vermont Network Against Domestic Violence and Sexual Assault
P.O. Box 405
Montpelier, VT 05601
phone: 802-223-1302
fax: 802-223-6443
Web site: www.vtnetwork.org

Virginians Aligned Against Sexual Assault
508 Dale Avenue, Suite B
Charlottesville, VA 22903
phone: 434-979-9002
fax: 434-979-9003
Web site: www.vaasa.org

Women's Coalition of St. Croix
P.O. Box 222734
Christiansted–St. Croix, VI 00822
phone: 340-773-9272
fax: 340-773-9062
Web site: www.wcstx.com

Washington Coalition of Sexual Assault Programs
2415 Pacific Avenue, SE, #10-C
Olympia, WA 98501

phone: 360-754-7583
fax: 360-786-8707
Web site: www.wcsap.org

West Virginia Foundation for Rape Information and Services, Inc.
112 Braddock Street
Fairmont, WV 26554
phone: 304-366-9500
fax: 304-366-9501
Web site: www.fris.org

Wisconsin Coalition Against Sexual Assault
600 Williamson Street, Suite N-2
Madison, WI 53703

phone: 608-257-1516
fax: 608-257-2150
Web site: www.wcasa.org

Wyoming Coalition Against Domestic Violence and Sexual Assault
P.O. Box 236
409 South 4th Street
Laramie, WY 82073
phone: 307-755-0992
toll-free: 800-990-3877
fax: 307-755-5482
Web site:
www.users.qwest.net/~wyoming
coalition/index.htm

Suggested Reading

Hollies, Linda H. *Inner Healing for Broken Vessels: Seven Steps to a Woman's Way of Healing* (Nashville: Upper Room, 1992).

———. *Taking Back My Yesterdays* (Cleveland: Pilgrim Press, 1997).

Robinson, Lori S. *I Will Survive: The African-American Guide to Healing from Sexual Assault and Abuse* (New York: Seal Press, 2002).

Weems, Renita. *Battered Love: Marriage, Sex, and Violence in the Hebrew Prophets* (Minneapolis: Fortress Press, 1995).

———. *I Asked for Intimacy: Stories of Blessings, Betrayals, and Birthings* (Philadelphia: Innisfree Press, 1993).

West, Traci C. *Wounds of the Spirit: Black Women, Violence, and Resistance Ethics* (New York: New York University Press, 1999).

Sexuality Education

The Sexuality Information and Education Council of the United States (SIECUS)
SIECUS Main Office
130 West 42nd Street, Suite 350
New York, NY 10036-7802
phone: 212-819-9770
fax: 212-819-9776
e-mail: siecus@siecus.org
SIECUS is a national, nonprofit organization affirming that sexuality is a natural and healthy part of living. Incorporated in 1964, SIECUS develops, collects, and disseminates information; promotes comprehensive education about sexuality; and advocates the right of individuals to make responsible sexual choices.

Preschool Curricula for Faith Communities

In God's Imagery
Janet Neff Brewer
A program for parents and their children ages 3–5 (Presbyterian), 1998; children's book $14.95; guide for parents $7.95; guide for congregations $6.95. Presbyterian Distribution Service, 100 Witherspoon Street, Louisville, KY 40202-1396; phone: 800-524-2612; fax: 502-569-8030; Web site: http://www.pcusa.org/pcusa/currpub

Elementary School Curricula
for Faith Communities

**Created by God: About Human Sexuality for
Older Girls and Boys**
Dorlis Brown Glass
A six-session curriculum for older elementary school children
(United Methodist), 1999; leader's guide $6.95; student book
$3.50. Cokesbury, 201 8th Avenue South, P.O. Box 801,
Nashville, TN 37202-0801; phone: 800-672-1789; fax: 800-445-
8189; Web site: http://www.cokesbury.org

Preventing Child Sexual Abuse
Ages 5–8
Kathryn Goering Reid
Ages 9–12
Kathryn Goering Reid with Marie M. Fortune
These two curricula provide information about sexual abuse and
prevention (UCC), 1994, ages 5–8, $9.95; 1989, ages 9–12,
$11.95. United Church Press, 700 Prospect Avenue, Cleveland,
OH 44115-1100; phone: 800-537-3394; fax: 216-736-3713; Web
site: http://www.ucc.org

Middle School/High School Curricula
for Faith Communities

A Course of Study for Teenagers
Rebecca Voelkel-Haugen and Marie M. Fortune
This curriculum for teenagers covers sexual abuse and
harassment (UCC), 1996; $8.95. United Church Press, 700
Prospect Avenue, Cleveland, OH 44115-1100; phone: 800-537-
3394; fax: 216-736-3713; Web site: http://www.ucc.org

Created in God's Image: A Human Sexuality Program for Ministry and Mission
Overview: Faith A. Johnson and Gordon J. Svoboda II
Leader's manual: Eleanor S. Morrison and Melanie Morrison
Participant's book: Melanie Morrison and Eleanor S. Morrison
A Manual for Ministry in the Congregation: Mary Ellen Haines and Bill Stackhouse
This program is written for college-aged youths and adults (UCC), 1993. Available with training. Contact Ann Hanson for more information at 216-736-3282; Division of the American Missionary Association, United Church Board for Homeland Ministries, 700 Prospect Avenue, Cleveland, OH 44115-1110.

Dating: The Art of Respect
Debbie Eisenbise and Lee Krahenbuhl
A middle school and high school curriculum (Church of the Brethren and the Mennonite Church), 1998; $14.95.
Faith & Life Resources, P.O. Box 347, Newton, KS 67114; phone: 800-743-2484; fax: 316-283-0454; Web site: http://www2.southwind.net/~gcmc/flp

In God's Image: Male and Female
Patricia Martens Miller
A human sexuality program for grades 5–8. Teacher's manuals, videos, student and parent worksheets, and additional materials are available for each grade (Catholic), 1989; teacher's manual $10.00. Flannery Company, 13123 Arrowspace Drive, Victorville, CA 92394; phone: 800-456-3400; fax: 800-284-5600.

Keeping It Real: A Faith-Based Model for Teen Dialogue on Sex and Sexuality

A seven-session program for teenagers developed by the Black Church Initiative of the Religious Coalition for Reproductive Choice. It consists of a facilitator's guide and a teen activity book, 2000; no fee. Religious Coalition for Reproductive Choice, 1025 Vermont Avenue NW, Suite 1130, Washington, DC 20005; phone: 202-628-7700; fax: 202-628-7716; Web site: http://www.rcrc.org

Let's Be Real: Honest Discussions About Faith and Sexuality

Duane A. Ewers and M. Stevens Games, editors

This nondenominational Christian curriculum is designed for adolescents in middle school and high school. It consists of six sessions of discussions on anatomy, decision making, relationships, contraception, sexually transmitted diseases, and media and culture. A parent resource is included, 1998; $20.00. Abingdon Press, 201 8th Avenue South, P.O. Box 801, Nashville, TN 37202-0801; phone: 800-251-3320; fax: 800-836-7802; Web site: http://www.abingdon.org

Our Whole Lives (OWL): A Lifespan Sexuality Education Series

OWL is a comprehensive lifespan sexuality education series developed jointly by the Unitarian Universalist Association and the United Church Board for Homeland Ministries. The series includes OWL grades K-1, OWL grades 4-6, OWL grades 7-9, OWL grades 10-12, OWL adults, a parent's guide, an advocacy manual, and accompanying guides on OWL and faith for each grade level. Information about the program can be found at the

Web site of the Unitarian Universalist Association (Unitarian Universalist Association and United Church of Christ). Call for prices for each level. Unitarian Universalist Association, UUA Bookstore, 25 Beacon Street, Boston, MA 02108; phone: 800-215-9076; fax: 617-723-4805; Web site: http://www.uua.org

For the Little Eves

Girls Inc.
Girls Incorporated
120 Wall Street
New York, NY 10005-3902
phone: 800-374-4475
Web site: www.girlsinc.org
There are numerous organizations dedicated to nurturing girls to full adulthood as positive, healthy, self-loving young women. Dr. Joyce Roché, President and CEO of Girls Incorporated, is doing just that. Girls Inc. is a national nonprofit youth organization dedicated to inspiring all girls "to be strong, smart, and bold." With roots dating to 1864, Girls Inc. has provided vital educational programs to millions of American girls, particularly those in high-risk, underserved areas. Today, innovative programs help girls confront subtle societal messages about their value and potential, and prepare them to lead successful, independent, and fulfilling lives. Girls Inc. develops research-based informal education programs that encourage girls to take risks and master physical, intellectual, and emotional challenges. Their programs address math and science education, pregnancy and drug abuse prevention, media literacy, economic literacy, adolescent health, violence prevention, and sports participation.

Rest and Renewal

Spa Finders
phone: 800-255-7727
An agency that specializes in identifying spa vacations
for any budget.

Suggested Readings

Muller, Wayne. *Sabbath: Finding Rest, Renewal, and Delight in Our Busy Lives* (New York: Bantam Books, 1999).

Taylor, Mikki. *Self-Seduction: Your Ultimate Path to Inner and Outer Beauty* (New York: Ballantine, 2003).

Williams, Terrie. *A Plentiful Harvest: Creating Balance and Harmony Through the Seven Living Virtues* (New York: Warner, 2002).

ABOUT THE AUTHOR

THE REVEREND DR. SUSAN NEWMAN, an ordained minister for the past twenty-eight years and a nationally recognized preacher and speaker, is the author of *With Heart and Hand: The Black Church Working to Save Black Children* and *Oh God! A Black Woman's Guide to Sex and Spirituality*. In addition, she is senior adviser to the mayor for religious affairs in Washington, DC.